THE SELF-MANAGEMENT PSYCHOLOGY SERIES
Carl E. Thoresen, Ph.D., *general editor*,
Stanford University

This series of self-help books presents techniques that really work based on scientifically sound research.

Designed with the layman in mind, each book presents a step-by-step method you can readily apply to solve real problems you confront in everyday life. Each is written by a respected behavioral scientist who has achieved success in applying these same techniques.

OTHER BOOKS IN THE SERIES:

Helen Brandhorst Krumboltz

GETTING THERE

Taking Charge for Personal Change

Prentice-Hall, Inc., Englewood Cliffs, New Jersey 07632

Library of Congress Cataloging in Publication Data

Krumboltz, Helen Brandhorst.
  Getting there.

  (The Self-management psychology series)
  "A Spectrum Book."
  Includes index.
    1. Women—Psychology.   2. Self-help techniques.
I. Title.   II. Series.
HQ1206.K77 1985   158'.1'Q88042   84-22307
ISBN 0-13-354945-3
ISBN 0-13-354937-2 (pbk.)

1 2 3 4 5 6 7 8 9 10

ISBN 0-13-354945-3

ISBN 0-13-354937-2 (PBK.)

Editorial/production supervision by Elizabeth Torjussen
Cover design © 1985 by Jeannette Jacobs
Manufacturing buyer: Anne P. Armeny

This book is available at a special discount when ordered in
bulk quantities. Contact Prentice-Hall, Inc., General
Publishing Division, Special Sales, Englewood Cliffs, N.J. 07632.

Prentice-Hall International, Inc., *London*
Prentice-Hall of Australia Pty. Limited, *Sydney*
Prentice-Hall Canada Inc., *Toronto*
Prentice-Hall Hispanoamericana, S.A., *Mexico*
Prentice-Hall of India Private Limited, *New Delhi*
Prentice-Hall of Japan, Inc., *Tokyo*
Prentice-Hall of Southeast Asia Pte. Ltd., *Singapore*
Whitehall Books Limited, *Wellington, New Zealand*
Editora Prentice-Hall do Brasil Ltda., *Rio de Janeiro*

Contents

Preface

This is a personal book. It is about women we all might know, but primarily it is about you, the reader, for it is a book that deals with self-change.

If I were to label the fields of knowledge from which the ideas are drawn, I would be quick to name psychology, because of its emphasis on social learning and cognitive restructuring methods; then immediately I would add sociology, women's studies, and education, because of contributions from these areas to potential self-change projects relevant to girls and women.

In my writing, however, I have worked hard *not* to be textbookish and to eliminate academic jargon, because I really want to reach *any* woman who wishes to find out more about herself and her surroundings and any man who shares this desire. While we are all affected by the women's movement, I hope not only to touch women whose lives are caught up in it but those who live more traditionally. People *can* change and grow at any age and in many different ways. This fact is attested to by the diversity of personal goals pursued by the women in these pages.

Research-based methods from behavioral psychology are represented by ten basic principles. Following an introductory chapter that tells you about them in a general way, these individual principles make up the backbone of the three major sections of the book: "Removing Blocks to Personal Change" (Chapters

2–5), "Building Your Own Kind of Life" (Chapters 6–8), and "Discarding Habits That Slow You Down" (Chapters 9–13). Scores of examples illustrate ways in which women use these principles in their everyday lives, and twenty small projects guide you in applying them to your own life.

The idea for a book focusing these psychological principles on a wide range of women's socialization issues came about for two reasons. The first was the writing of a book, *Changing Children's Behavior,* with John D. Krumboltz (Prentice-Hall, 1972), in which the original form of the principles was spelled out. It was at a time when momentum for the women's movement was growing and practical applications of behavioral psychology began to appear in the form of books on self-control and assertion. The second was a logical follow-up—my teaching of a course at Stanford University in which the principles were adapted to a self-change model, then extended and applied to specific ways women could change their own actions. The format has since expanded in several directions: applications to specialized groups of women of various ages, increased treatment of men's roles, gender issues related to business management, and training workshops for professionals.

Students' ideas enliven many topics you will read about, and I enthusiastically acknowledge their constructive suggestions and personal support. I especially wish to mention Sidney T. Brown, Gretchen Dennison, Nina Farana, Kalayanee Srifuengfung, Debbie Then, and Tere Valdeś.

I am grateful to these Stanford faculty and staff for their special interest: Elizabeth Cohen, Leah Kaplan, Myra Strober, David Tyack, and Carl Thoresen, the editor of this series. I also thank Mary E. Pike for generous assistance during a three-year period and acknowledge the long-standing support of the Stanford Center for Research on Women.

Discussions with Johanna Shapiro helped clarify certain points and raise new ones in portions of Chapters 1 to 3.

There are others who helped make this task possible, plausible, or pleasant: Eunice and Otto Brandhorst; Margaret Gage; Juliette George; Ann, Jennifer, and John Krumboltz; Dan and Mary Jane Rolfs; Lenore Seltzer; and Gilbert Wrenn.

Not least, my appreciation to those whose skills were vital

in the manuscript countdown: Connie Barrell, Ruth Bergman, Daphne Hamilton, Mary Johnson, and Helen Nash.

Helen Brandhorst Krumboltz lectures to groups on gender issues and conducts seminars for professionals. For more than ten years she has taught gender-related self-management courses to Stanford University undergraduate and graduate students and has run workshops for specialized groups of women. She is the co-author of *Changing Children's Behavior* (Prentice-Hall, 1972).

To John
and
to Ann and Jen

Part 1

ORIGINS

Make yourself comfortable. Find a good chair and a quiet spot. Imagine that you have a chance to talk to an old friend, someone you can trust. The women described in this book believe in women, and they are learning to believe and trust in themselves. They want to share their thinking with you. They know we have common destinies and common origins. Each one, in her own way, is *getting there*.

CHAPTER ONE

Roots and Rationale

Her grandmother and great-grandmother, strong
women in their own rights, served as her role models.
She is said to have been her father's favorite child.
Even her grandfather championed a higher status for
women. Her name was Hatshepsut, and she ruled Egypt
for eighteen years, from 1486 B.C. to 1468 B.C., by
seizing power and proclaiming herself—king.*

Our interest lies in our todays and tomorrows, but present-
day perspective grows out of the past, both recent and ancient.
Hatshepsut's life is that of a woman leader of renowned beauty,
with women role models, an encouraging father, and an enlightened family. It is the life of an ambitious, pragmatic
woman who understands she cannot change her society to
rule it as a queen, so she arranges an alternative way to gain
control over her world by changing her own image into that
of a man and becoming its king. In doing so she is able to
rule legitimately as a god. Her good works are strikingly

*This composite description of Hatshepsut derives from several sources.
For one account of this woman see Evelyn Well's *Hatshepsut*. New York:
Doubleday, 1969.

familiar—developing building enterprises and foreign trade, and constructing a beautifully terraced temple which, however, did not contain a library to document her reign.

Hatshepsut would understand many of the issues mentioned within the scope of this book but would surely be surprised at the range of life styles for women today. Let's take a capsule look at seven contemporary women.

Seven Sisters: Profiles in Our Time

KRISTIN

Kristin's straight dark-blonde hair falls to her shoulders. Of medium height, she admits she would like to lose the ten pounds she gained during child-bearing, but in her daily attire of blue jeans and loose tops, the extra weight she worries about is not apparent. Kristin loves children, and at age twenty-nine she is married and has three under five years of age. "At first it was terribly exciting to watch a tiny human being develop. Everything was new, and sometimes the responsibility was really scary. But after the third time around I am beginning to feel, well, not really trapped, because I love kids, but I do feel a twinge of dissatisfaction about my life in contrast to Andy's exciting one. After he leaves for work in the morning it's the worst. I face the clean-up and supervision of three little kids all day long. By the time he returns home in the evening I sometimes greet him with crossed eyes saying 'nanoo nanoo nanoo.' But when he grabs me and says, 'Krissy, you're a wonderful mother,' everything seems okay again." Kristin seeks out other mothers with small children and tries to read "something worthwhile" when the children nap, "but oftentimes either *I* fall asleep or they *don't.*"

Kristin does not know what she will do when the children are all in school. "But," she says, "recently my four-year-old daughter said to me, 'I don't want to be a mommy when I grow up. I want to be *me*,' and that really made me wonder about myself."

VALERIE

Thirty-seven-year-old Valerie claims, "My life seems to be one continuous challenge to cope rather than to cop out." Her piercing gray eyes are a clue to Val's intensity and intelligence. She wears her long, naturally wavy hair tied back, as a way to reduce her preparation time in the mornings. As a wife, mother, and attorney, Valerie knows well the meaning of role overload. She has no patience with other women who "can't seem to get their act together." As for friends, she has little time for either sex but considers a number of acquaintances "associates." When pinned down she admits she prefers men to women because she considers them "more honest."

Although her husband does help "about 15 percent of the time" with their children, Val wants to make certain she does not sacrifice time with them for time on her legal work. Although she arranges daily after-school baby-sitting for her two children in elementary school, she also blocks out time on a daily and weekend basis for them and claims they are better off not being pampered. "No guilt trip here." But she does experience nagging moments of concern about her relationship with her husband when the two of them go for extended periods of time on what she refers to as "a crisis communication schedule."

Valerie sets high standards for herself in all her roles and tries hard to balance them, even when admitting that sometimes her high expectations get in the way of her actual performance. "My one fear," she sums up, "is that I won't be strong enough to hang on to all this, and that I might run down like a battery from too much use."

LEXY

As an assistant manager in a company supplying office services, Lexy, at age forty-one, dresses casually in her job, and except for flecks of gray hair, has the overall demeanor of a person a generation younger. She likes to downplay her appearance. Lexy is not married and feels men have provoked many of women's problems, but she also feels "a lot of us simply don't get out there and push ourselves enough because it makes us uncomfortable. Then we aren't acknowledged. It reminds me of when I was helping a friend's husband replace two windowpanes under the eave of their house. It was hard work, but we got the job done. Then, instead of appreciating me as a physically strong person for the job, he told me 'Now you see why I needed a man to help.' I was furious and felt like kicking his ladder over but said nothing. Once again, a woman's job ignored."

Raised by her mother to work at "just about everything," Lexy hopes to save enough money to buy herself a van and start a business helping people with repair jobs such as the one just mentioned. "I would like to demonstrate how good I am, with no connection to whether I'm young or beautiful. Men call women vain, but when we grow up getting clues that we must be pretty in order to succeed at anything, what can they expect? It really makes me angry."

ANGIE

Angie, age nineteen, is five feet two-and-one-half inches tall with eyes of blue-green. When asked what she considers her major asset, she answers without hesitation that it is her golden hair. A community college student, she does well in the biological sciences but claims her real college specialty is "relationships." Her zest for living centers around close friendships with two girl friends and a string of boyfriends about her age.

About women in general she says, "I like them and really don't feel competitive," but she is bothered by those who resort to " 'airheadism'—being a little kooky around the guys." She herself prefers not to compete with men and admits she "almost feels like apologizing" if she finds herself beating them in badminton or making higher grades. Angie recognizes that this attitude is inconsistent with her belief that women and men are equal, and then she laughingly goes on to describe how she always pays her own way to movies but really loves it when her current boyfriend makes the decisions about what they will do together.

She says she expects that her future will take care of

itself, and when asked to clarify what she means by "future," she mentions later college years and finding a man she wants to marry. But Angie can be contemplative, even philosophical, and when she is serious, she wonders how she will ever use her education. "My mom was lucky. In her day there weren't so many choices. Now it's pretty overwhelming."

CYNTHIA

At forty-seven, Cynthia says, "Yes, I have what I want in life." Cynthia and her husband, Charlie, who is sixteen years her senior, live in a suburban home with three garages, a Jacuzzi, a twice-monthly cleaning service, and a burglar alarm system. Cynthia won a local beauty contest when she was a teenager and continues to try hard to maintain her figure by working out three times a week in a local dance class. Their one child, a daughter, was born when Cynthia was twenty and now lives in her own apartment.

Charlie takes Cynthia on frequent business trips to New York, where they enjoy the high life, dining in expensive restaurants and attending the theater. Then during the day, while he conducts business, she shops, keeping herself abreast of the latest clothes, hair, and cosmetic fashions. "He likes me to look good for his clients." "He" is Charlie. Cynthia consistently refers to him not by his name but by an appropriate masculine pronoun.

When asked if she feels as if she plays a shadow role or is primarily an ornament for her husband, Cynthia immediately counters: "I like a straight world where all the glasses match. I can have that with him. So he doesn't ever ask my opinion. He does ignore me, but he also adores me. Once in a while I wonder what would happen if he suddenly died or something like that, but nobody knows what will happen in the future."

LORRAINE

At age seventy-four, Lorraine is a handsome woman. With short, carefully groomed white hair, alert brown eyes, and tan skin, she radiates vitality but complains, "I have no place to go."

Lorraine lives alone. Her three married children live in other states. Before her husband's death several years ago, the two of them bought a second-hand camper and enjoyed several trips around the country together. Now her friends are limited entirely to the women with whom she plays canasta, and she regrets not finding the means to establish social contacts with men. Lorraine states unabashedly, "I love men."

She would like to enlarge her circle of friends and interests. "Like so many women I know, I lived many years through my husband. But that doesn't mean I don't have some spunk in me. I do have a brain I can still use."

Lorraine feels an absence of a place in society for women in her time of life. She quotes a friend who told her, "We are not so much *mis*understood as *un*-understood." By way of explanation she adds, "I don't think anyone is really *against* me, but at my age is anyone really *for* me? Can a woman maintain credibility at seventy-four?"

SHERRY

Tall and lanky at fifty-five, Sherry looks the essence of responsibility. Divorced for five years and the sole support of two adolescent children, her face shows the care and concern she feels in her role as mother. Clerking with her at the grocery store where she works is her "significant other," a man who wants to move in with her; she worries, however, about the example this would set for her children, as well as the changes that would occur in family relationships.

Sherry can best be described as a "rock." Although she is accustomed to a busy schedule, she manages to give both her children and her male companion strong emotional support, and in their own ways they all lean on her. Raised as the eldest child in a close family, she has had long experience shouldering responsibility. All the same, she still feels the heavy burden of mothering two teenagers in an era of drugs and casual sex.

Though the women's movement is not one of her priorities, Sherry occasionally stops to ask herself some questions about the life she leads as a woman. Concerned about her

8

own kids making good grades in school, she comments, "But what I want to know is, how do *I* get an A in *life?*"

Like the rest of us, the women just profiled are both typical and atypical. They represent various life styles and ages. Each possesses strengths, reflects her socialization, and is not without human weaknesses. Their concerns and desires are much like any other woman's whom you will read about shortly. These are summarized in the following list.

WHAT ISSUES ARE IMPORTANT TO YOU?
1. To relate to the opposite sex as a person rather than as a sex object, never using your gender to manipulate others, so that you in turn will be treated as a person and not be manipulated as a sex object.
2. To relate to your own sex with respect and dignity, even when realizing that you will find few role models to help you in any quest for increased personal identity.
3. To become skilled in problem-solving and decision-making, knowing that the more you are comfortable relying on your own judgment and able to take carefully planned risks, the more you will be your own person.
4. To seek appropriate outlets for feelings of anger resulting from society's inequities and to exercise judgment about when and how to be assertive.
5. To encourage yourself to achieve up to your potential without feeling guilty when you do not attain perfection; when you do excel, to understand the possibility of rejection from either women or men because of your accomplishments.
6. To cultivate your particular interests without regard to sex or age stereotyping.
7. To find confidence in your own abilities and skills when unacknowledged because of your earlier socialization or when rusty from lack of use.
8. To place in perspective the goals you have in life, analyze their ramifications, and plan what actions on your part will help you to implement them without putting unrealistic demands on yourself or on those you love.
9. To persist and be ingenious in applying for school, a job, or a promotion when you suspect disguised prejudice against what you represent (female: wrong color, somebody's relative, no raving beauty, too young or too old, divorced, part-time, have

children, too straight or too counter-culture) rather than appreciation for what skills, talents, or experiences you offer.

10. To explore ways to make child-rearing less burdensome and more rewarding, at the same time retaining your parental responsibility.

11. To tolerate resistance from your family, children, or mate if you change your living pattern, realizing that a change by any member is bound to require an adjustment from each of the others.

12. To remember that when a man finds the sharing of his world difficult, it is not necessarily due to his own imperfections but to the same culture that conditioned you, and that he needs the security of understanding how he too will profit from conditions that open up more options for you both.

13. To realize that little by little through your own everyday actions you create your personal destiny, just as surely as your life is influenced by its major events.

Some of the concerns mentioned may not apply to you. Perhaps you have already found certain solutions. But given our gender role socialization and today's world, it is difficult to imagine any woman who, after searching within herself, can honestly say she has everything figured out and feels completely satisfied with the way she is. Like Hatshepsut, we become our own image-builders.

Behavioral Self-Change: The Means to Move Ahead

SETTING DIRECTIONS

The examples and insights from women in the pages that follow support their objectives and our own; namely, to

- increase self-awareness (personal identity)
- increase control of personal responses (autonomy)
- increase positive personal feelings (self-esteem)
- decrease feelings of guilt and hostility
- increase the ability to relate effectively to others

Behavioral self-change offers us the means to move ahead in these directions.

UNDERSTANDING THE BASICS

These underlying notions are significant to what we will discuss:

Behavioral self-change is not just a matter of willpower. Systematically developed, research-based tools from psychology, stated in the form of principles, help us increase self-awareness and understand the diverse and often subtle influences of our surroundings. As our competence in the use of the principles grows, not only do the reasons for past actions become more clear but we are able to exercise more control over our future behavior.

People don't need to feel differently before acting differently. At one time people believed that feelings needed to be altered before a person's actions could change. Now we know it can happen either way. If we change our actions, changes in our feelings usually are not far behind.

Most attitudes and actions are learned. This includes how we value ourselves and how we respond to others. We know that only a fraction of our learning is formal—that is, openly planned by parents, schools, or religious institutions. Most of it is informal, stemming from many sources—including our imitation of others and how we sense people respond to us. It is this informal "hidden" education that so often works against women in our society.

What people learn can be systematically unlearned—or improved upon. Behavioral self-change offers skills that help us stop habits that hold us back and increase those that we prefer. All together they become the foundation of a more positive self-view, enabling us to value ourselves more. Competence then becomes not only a set of skills but a state of mind.

The changes are self-determined. Our book draws heavily on other women's ideas that we consider relevant, so you can select the changes you desire from a wider range of options than your own personal experiences. But *you* do the selecting. What changes you want are up to you. Only when *you* make the decisions will your incentive to follow through be strong.

People can and do change at any age. We don't grow up, marry, and live happily ever after. We become physically mature, may or may not marry, and inevitably face challenges for change and growth until we die. We do not necessarily become set in our ways. Throughout our lives we continuously make decisions that lead us toward or away from flexibility and positive growth.

KNOWING THE ADVANTAGES

There are special reasons why the methods of behavioral self-change are attractive to women.

Women learn skills to increase personal control over their lives. The ways we formulate and act upon alternative patterns of action help us move from passive to active and from dependent to self-reliant, gaining more personal control and competence as we go along.

Women learn the environmental context of their concerns. We find that our problems are not necessarily unique or self-caused, and that our frustration and guilt often flow from our surroundings rather than from personal flaws. Women, for example, sometimes experience guilt due to aging. Increased years can bring a sense of personal failure because of our youth-oriented culture, in which women especially (but men, too) are looked upon with increasingly less favor as they grow older. In some cultures age represents wisdom and is revered, but rarely is this the case in ours. As we realize that the fault lies in our culture and not in ourselves, we are able to view aging more realistically and know that others share the same problem.

Behavioral self-change is a positive approach. With women's socialization toward nurturance our task is simple—to make use of our nurturing qualities in additional ways. We do not wish to be punitive; there are advantages to coping without being punishing to ourselves or to others.

KNOWING THE LIMITATIONS

Focusing primarily on issues common in everyday life, the solutions found by women within these pages may well be therapeutic but are not intended to replace therapy. We try to stay away from potentially deep-seated problems such as alcoholism, agoraphobia, severe depression, *anorexia nervosa*, or sexual malfunction. Other sources already deal with these important issues in depth. Our major interest is our socialization.

Behavioral self-change promises few quick solutions and no sensational answers. Although we speculate occasionally about reasons for failures to assure you that the principles do not represent only apple pie and motherhood, successes are clearly more evident. This is not only because they give us more joy but because the methods, when used properly, do indeed work most of the time.

One additional thing you should know: The pages ahead heavily reflect middle-class living patterns because most of the women happen to come from this segment of our population. We also recognize inherent stereotypes about women that may not be fully justified, such as an emphasis on nurturance when women are not always nurturing (and for that matter that many men certainly are). Finally, the case material throughout is based on deliberately camouflaged experiences and no actual names are mentioned.

GETTING STARTED

These instructions will serve as final thoughts as you begin:

Expect resistance. Yes, from others, but especially from yourself. Sameness is a cushion. Say to yourself, "Change makes all of us a little hesitant. It's normal."

Allow room for mistakes. Many women want success assured or they won't try. Ask yourself what you can afford to risk. Then be prepared to lose a little for the possibility of gaining a lot.

Stay alert for self-deception. Sometimes our private betrayals are so successful that we don't bother to question whether we are letting ourselves down. Remember to be on the lookout for the possibility of shaping, through many small acts of your own, a life you don't want. *Think:* "Does this action contribute to or detract from the person I want to become?"

Kristin, Valerie, Lexy, Angie, Cynthia, Lorraine, Sherry— all are contemporary women with the usual range of problems and successes. Fortunately for them, to live life to the fullest they do not need to change their image to that of a man as Hatshepsut did. In today's world each has the opportunity to create for herself the image she wants—as a woman. The same is true for the rest of us.

Part 2

REMOVING BLOCKS TO PERSONAL CHANGE

Let's focus first on ways to remove the obstacles in our paths.

You begin in Chapter two by learning how to make goals realistic and reasonable in order to go to work on them. In Chapter three you'll see how to obtain an outsider's view of yourself, clarifying who you really are and what are your choices. Do you ever think much about your personal pleasures? Many women don't. But you will when you read Chapter four. Then in Chapter five you will see how to face up to everyday fears and stresses that block the directions you want to take next.

CHAPTER TWO

Target Practice:
The First Step

One thing I know: I want to grow—to be my own person. But what does that *mean*? When I don't know who I am, how do I *find* me?

Lucy

I know what I want for myself. But *getting* from here to there. . . ! It's like flying in fog without radar.

Maryann

You know the feeling. That heightened awareness about who you are and the impact of surrounding events on your life. For one woman it emerges from the wistfulness and inadequacy she feels after talking to a friend who opens a plant shop that is "really on its way." It often arises when a divorce catapults a homemaker into the full-time labor force for her economic survival, or when a woman manager analyzes why she is passed over for promotion. Sometimes it accompanies the fear a graduating senior experiences when she wonders whether she can live up to her Superwoman ideals. Or it may surface simply from the question, "Why do I have such a sense of power when my husband is away on a business trip?" We do not refer to these feelings as a "raised consciousness" because they do not constitute a completed state. Rather, they are part of a continuing, growing awareness, gradually revealing to each of us more about ourselves and our world.

Reactions to Increasing Awareness

Occasionally, by luck or wisdom, the changes a woman initiates as a result of increasing awareness are performed smoothly and efficiently, with her life apparently falling into a neat new niche. She is alive and well and becoming her own person. But more often, women seeking to understand where they are today—women with sensitivity, savvy, and even abounding inner strength—still find it difficult to translate their new awareness into personal actions that will bring them the results they yearn for. Most of us will recognize ourselves in at least some of the following reactions because they have been part of our own growth process. But take a look at ways they can hold us back.

THE SYMBOLIC REACTION

Superficial overtures mark the reactions of one type of woman who may experience difficulty. She may be prone to make an issue about opening her own car door, or may even legally change her last name from *Jack*son to *Ruth*daughter. It would be unfair to suggest that a person taking such actions does so only to display in a shallow way her growing awareness. These can be courageous acts, but they are truly inadequate if regarded as sufficient changes by themselves.

THE ALL-OR-NOTHING REACTION

The all-or-nothing reaction occurs when a woman attempts total change in large areas of her life but at the same time cuts herself off from much that has previously been of value to her. She may decide to leave not only her husband but her children, friends, and job as well. This is sometimes known as the "from-now-on-I'm-going-to-lead-my-own-life-and-to-hell-with-everyone-else" stance. For this woman the high risk is in trading off her old support system for a new life she has not yet built.

THE TUNNEL VISION REACTION

Another overreaction occurs with the hard-core do-or-die women's libber who decides that the radical approach is the Only Way and acts out her own scenario accordingly. About one such woman someone observed, "She turns just about everything *anybody* does into a sexist act." Tunnel vision fervor avoids compromise with either sex. It demands attention, but others often question what a woman with this reaction hopes to accomplish.

THE GLOBAL RAGE REACTION

Sometimes an angry woman, ridden with frustration as injustices from her socialization in a male-oriented society become clear to her, strikes out with cutting aggression in an attempt to get even. So we hear, "What do you expect from a male chauvinist pig?" or read a chain letter suggesting bundling up a husband and sending him to the top of the list with advice not to break the chain. ("One woman did and got her husband back.") Humor is tainted with biting sarcasm and jarring wit, prompting the question: Is there any way we can keep our sense of humor but focus anger more constructively?

THE OVERREACTION TO OVERREACTION

Overreaction often occurs when a woman responds to others' tunnel vision or rage. Her antagonism is demonstrated by an unwillingness to be identified in any way with the women's movement. She declares herself strongly against the major issues. A pity, for the turned-off woman not only has much to offer but much to gain.

THE HELPLESSNESS REACTION

"I'll never be able to change." "I can't do it on my own." "It's too late for me." Feeling powerless and overwhelmed by her new awareness, a woman voicing these sentiments paradoxically often displays even more passivity and dependence. Result: She is unhappy with herself, and this can surface in dissatisfaction with those around her. Negativism and depression lurk like storm clouds in the sky.

These reactions illustrate that as our awareness increases we may unwittingly limit ourselves further in our attempts to change. For this reason we need to examine carefully the directions we wish to take and make certain we translate them into constructive steps for personal growth.

Global Goals

Hopes and dreams we have for ourselves are really global goals. Increased awareness often results in women talking about personal desires such as being more independent, coping better, or becoming less depressed. These are global goals, as are the ones stated in Chapter one for helping women set directions: to increase autonomy, self-esteem, and personal identity, to reduce guilt and hostility, and to relate more effectively to others. Global goals are always broad and visionary, and as such they can serve as useful starting points. So, before you read further, think about your own global goals for the first *Time for Yourself* project.

Time for Yourself #1

Identify and write down two global goals of your own.

1. _____

2. _____

Although they are useful to convey large general ideas, global goals lack substance because they are not stated in operational terms. Speculating on her private life, Sue complains to her friends, "The trouble with me is that I need to be more self-reliant." Now her friends may well have some hint of what Sue means by self-reliance but probably little idea about what she would do to attain it. Chances are, Sue doesn't know either. Women often become stuck on global goals because they find them difficult to convert into action. Old habits remain when we don't know exactly what steps to take next. So global goals, though openers, need to be recognized and labeled for the abstractions they are.

To start a self-change project, proceed quickly to more solid ground. Your next move: Bring each visionary goal down to a level that you can think and talk about, and eventually work on, in behavioral terms.

The relationship between goal levels need not be lost, however: "I'm working on this job-sharing resumé because I believe part-time work will give me more financial freedom." The connection between a global goal (in this case, financial freedom) and your own immediate action is always there if you wish to make it. Indeed, sometimes retaining that link in your mind adds a sense of accomplishment to the simpler acts you perform to attain those larger goals.

Starter Goals

Recall that Sue spoke to her friends about wanting to become more self-reliant. Joan now asks, "But, Sue, come on. What are you talking about? What does self-reliance mean to you?"
They exchange ideas.

SUE: To me, self-reliance means *not depending on others to handle my financial matters* or *planning time on my own to carry out some project.*

JOAN: Well, as far as I'm concerned it means *being able to come and go as I wish, perhaps with a car of my own,* or *feeling I can speak up easily when I disagree with someone's opinion.*

Sue's other friends add their own examples of self-reliance:

JEAN: *Taking on new responsibilities that I decide on for myself.*

LOU: *Being able to disagree without becoming angry.*

JAN: *Doing my best rather than always letting guys win at games.*

21

The working definitions these women give represent seven starter goals. Notice each is a *description* of action that can be *observed* and no longer an intangible idea. Each specifies changes these women might make in themselves in relation to their surroundings. **The Starter Goal Principle: To determine the action you want to take, restate a global goal in operational terms as several starter goals and then convert each starter goal into precise target behaviors you can work on in given situations.** Starter goals give you explicit ideas about what your global goals stand for before you convert them into the target behaviors that will be discussed later. Right now, starter goals deserve a closer look.

WHY STARTER GOALS?

To clarify where to begin. As Sue and her friends demonstrate, a starter goal points us in a particular direction. That's why they are called starter goals.

To know ourselves and our surroundings better. When searching for starter goals we look more closely at specific situations in our lives and in our personal environment. We observe ourselves and others. We think about our own needs, too. Maria, for example, is aware of her children's need for a quiet time and space of their own. But as she goes about arranging this for them, it occurs to her that she disregards her own need for exactly that same privacy, and that without it she does not cope as well with her children. Maria sees that it is not only permissible but necessary for her children's welfare to help herself as well as them. Her starter goal now is to arrange at least some degree of privacy both for her children *and* for herself.

To communicate with other women. With similar socialization, women have much to gain by sharing ideas with one another. Starter goals help us communicate with less ambiguity about change possibilities. When examined in the context of your own life, you may find that another woman's starter goal dovetails with your own needs so well that you incorporate it in your own change plans.

Take Laurie, for example. A high school senior, she listens to a classmate's starter goal; namely, to stop making favorable comments about other people's appearance—clothes, hairdo, complexion. "When I first heard it I thought, 'Wow, that's me all right.' I always comment on people's looks. What's wrong with that? But when I thought about it I decided I'd done it entirely too much because it leads others to believe looks are terribly important to me. I don't want people to think I'm hung up on superficial qualities. Girls and women *are* sometimes accused of this. So I simply stopped commenting on people's appearance. I like to compliment people but now I look for other ways." (Notice that once Laurie decides what she wants, her change is immediate and complete, without apparent effort. While most changes require more planning, occasionally they occur as easily as the flip of a switch.)

To recognize our own accomplishments. You will notice in others' starter goals areas where you already do well. That helps you identify your own strengths. Some women keep lists not only of starter goals they wish to work on but others they feel they have already achieved. In a group of young mothers sharing starter goals, one parent of two children under three called out, "Slow down, everybody! I get my week's best strokes each time I hear a starter goal I can record on my 'have dunnit' list, and right now I need all the encouragement I can get." Finding honest ways to give ourselves approval does wonders for our self-esteem.

To learn more about our own sex. As you are about to see, the search for starter goals extends into realms that enlarge our perspective about women. As we look more closely at the substance of female roles, we often find ourselves better able to identify with our own sex and less prone to judge women by the criteria of our male-oriented society.

FINDING PERSONAL STARTER GOALS

Demystifying global goals by citing "for instances" in operational terms is not the only way to arrive at starter goals. You will find them waiting to be uncovered under many other conditions. Here are some to explore.

Dick and Jane revisited. Read. Read almost anything—novels, contemporary women's magazines, history, current

For Better or For Worse

by Lynn Johnston

POTENTIAL STARTER GOAL: THANKS, BUT LESS THANKS

events—but with your mind set for starter goals. (Even comic strips instruct us.)

Newspapers are outstanding sources. Glancing through the daily paper you may run across an Erma Bombeck column about someone who can't just say goodbye and leave, money tips by Sylvia Porter, or an article interviewing people about how they react to praise. When you do, ask yourself: "Do I

24

hang around when I say goodbye?" "Have I established my own credit rating?" "Do I accept compliments easily?" (instead of saying "If you can open a can, you too can make this recipe," or "Larry liked it so I bought it—it was his idea, not mine.")

Children's literature is a rich source of information about your own background. Include books you knew yourself as a child, and don't forget those early Mother Goose rhymes. Look for implied as well as flagrant sex bias, both in stories and pictures. Notice that one girl needs a boy to bring a chair so she can stand on it to reach for peanut butter, while another is portrayed as passively watching her twin brother rescue a kitten in a tree. Ask yourself: "Is this part of my own 'hidden' education?" If so, don't stop when you realize it, or use it as an excuse for your own behavior. What starter goals can you work on to counteract that earlier socialization so you become a less dependent person?

Friendship feedback. Ask close friends to give their opinions of your three main strengths and weaknesses. Requesting both enables you to obtain feedback about your areas of competence as well as possible starter goals. Besides, people feel more comfortable offering a mixed rather than a negative evaluation.

Lynn: "Les, I'm supposed to ask someone to tell me three of my strengths and three of my weaknesses. I need some honest feedback and thought you'd be the person to ask." Les quickly comes up with three strengths: Lynn is easy to talk to, she's supportive of others, and she never brags about her hot-shot tennis game. As to weaknesses, well, she sometimes rides a subject pretty hard. Then, too, she is a tad sensitive to criticism. Finally, she does tend to put herself last, especially with her family. Lynn now has some solid ideas to work with.

Self-feedback. For at least a week, keep track in writing of despairing moments in your days—such as when you feel worried or wish you had acted differently. To trigger starter goal ideas, you might try completing sentences like "I am uncomfortable when. . . ," "I am afraid to. . . ," or "Why in the world do I. . . ," and in each instance describe how you would rather act. For example, "I am uncomfortable when I make a lot of excuses to my secretary about retyping jobs. After all, that's what he's paid for. Why don't I just matter-of-factly say I'd like to have him retype the letters?" Here comes a starter goal: "Stop making excuses for work I give my secretary."

Group insights. From planned meetings (formal support groups, special interest organizations, women's networks) to spontaneous get-togethers (rap sessions, coffee breaks), starter goals can be discussed and shared. But remember, the purpose is to arrive at constructive and creative change possibilities, not to have a gripe session.

Combinations. Starter goals often emerge from a mix of sources. Let's look again at Lynn, who identifies a starter goal for herself by using two sources: first her friend Les and then a support group. When her support group members discuss self-effacement in women, Lynn thinks back to the way she initially introduced herself to the group as "the wife of a computer programmer and the mother of a twelve-year-old boy." Suddenly she connects this introduction (showing her reliance on others for her identity) with what her friend Les told her about putting herself last. Lynn's starter goal: "Describe myself on my own merits." ("I'm Lynn. I love to cook gourmet meals.")

STARTER GOAL EXAMPLES

The starter goals that follow are derived from sources like those just mentioned by many women highly energized to keep growing. You will find them divided into three major self-change areas: handling fear or stress (Chapter five), encouraging desirable behaviors (Chapters six to nine), and stopping unwanted habits (Chapters ten to thirteen). Within each area the goals are further grouped (and sometimes quite arbitrarily so) under the global goals of our book. Since women have differing ideas, the goals are not equally specific, and sometimes they overlap or even contradict each other. All together they represent what these women feel are constructive directions to take—for them.

If you choose to read just one list at a given sitting, you will allow yourself time to check off those goals you think you have accomplished (or that don't interest you), to jot down other goals that occur to you (from reading these), and to ponder constructive directions to take—for you.

STARTER GOALS
FOR HANDLING FEAR OR STRESS

The following starter goals pertain to inhibitions these women want to overcome. They are stated as fears (or stresses) to work on.

OVERCOMING FEARS THAT LIMIT PERSONAL IDENTITY:
>   Looking/acting middle-aged or old
>   Not keeping an immaculately clean house
>   Making simple rather than elaborate meals for company
>   Being "too logical for a woman"
>   Being considered unfeminine
>   Being considered too sexy
>   Not being considered sexy enough
>   Being considered a tomboy
>   Showing real feelings; expressing how you really feel
>   Being ignored or feeling "invisible" in a group
>   Being "just a number, name, face, body, title (e.g., housewife)"

OVERCOMING FEARS THAT LIMIT SELF-ESTEEM:
>   Competing with others
>   Children not behaving well in public
>   Being rejected by a man you would like to know but don't want to sleep with
>   Losing a man who is a security object to you
>   Being considered ugly
>   Being liked only for your looks, money, or family background
>   Thwarting social interaction between males when you are the only female
>   Being ostracized by males because you are "too intellectual"
>   Being ostracized by males by competing with them and winning
>   Not making sense when you describe something
>   Defending yourself, as in an argument or disagreement
>   Being laughed at when you are different from the norm

OVERCOMING FEARS THAT LIMIT AUTONOMY:
  Taking a trip alone
  Eating alone in a restaurant
  Losing independence by marrying
  Being single or unattached
  Taking risks
  Making a "wrong" decision (and therefore making no decision)
  Completing school (getting a job, getting married, living alone)
  Driving a car in city traffic, on freeway, etc.
  Taking a taxi alone
  Applying for a job or school admission
  Supporting yourself financially
  Working with math, numbers
  Keeping a budget and not making errors
  Filing income tax forms
  Speaking in front of people, as in a class or meeting
  Directing or giving orders to others
  Working with mechanical devices

OVERCOMING FEARS THAT LIMIT CONTROL OF GUILT OR HOSTILITY:
  Not living up to others' expectations
  Hurting others
  "Dropping" people with whom there is little or nothing in
  common
  Not keeping others happy
  Being considered aggressive
  Damaging any male ego
  Turning someone down
  Pregnant pauses or silences in conversation

OVERCOMING FEARS THAT LIMIT RELATING EFFECTIVELY TO OTHERS:
  Not being allowed in your child's "space"
  Asking men out
  Asking men to dance
  Touching others, being touched
  Working for a woman, working for a man
  Meeting new people
  Joining a club or group

Speaking to strangers

Sharing responsibility with others

Asking questions of authority figures (teachers, physicians, auto mechanics)

STARTER GOALS
FOR ENCOURAGING DESIRABLE BEHAVIORS

These starter goals are for actions the women say they want to increase. They either wish to work on them from scratch or to encourage any positive tendencies that already exist.

STRENGTHENING ACTIONS THAT PROMOTE PERSONAL IDENTITY:

Acknowledging your own needs clearly to yourself and to others

Building your own individual support system, not just being a part of someone else's

Finding psychological/physical space for yourself

Setting priorities

Developing a support network with women in similar circumstances to yours so you can talk over issues and solutions

Living more in the present (rather than in the past or future)

Examining your own expectations against reality

Assessing your own attributes and limitations

Talking in a low, well-modulated voice

Strengthening your voice (using tape, talking through doors)

Giving directions as statements rather than as questions

Saying goodbye effectively and efficiently

Speaking precisely (without ambiguity)

Describing events briefly and coming to the point quickly; not repeating yourself

Assessing how you come across to others in nonverbal ways

Keeping conversation on issues (rather than your children, husband, boyfriend, job, etc.)

Recognizing cues to your own fatigue and responding to them

Developing a relaxed attitude of not expecting everything to go right

STRENGTHENING ACTIONS THAT PROMOTE SELF-ESTEEM:

Strengthening your positive socialized characteristics (e.g., caring, sensitivity)

Sharing responsibility for family decisions equally with your husband

Keeping score in athletics and table games

Contributing your share of conversation and question-asking, especially if group is male-dominated

Making up your own mind without relying unnecessarily on the opinions of others

Learning to live with a problem that cannot be changed (e.g., bad health, handicapped child)

Giving yourself positive feedback ("I did that well," "I'm doing better")

Trying new experiences: people, places, activities

Speaking up when needing help (as opposed to covering mistakes)

Stating an opinion honestly rather than trying first to second-guess what the other person wants to hear

Speaking forcefully when necessary

Accepting compliments easily and graciously

Becoming comfortable with lack of closure (e.g., learning it's okay not to complete all tasks)

Focusing on a job for the task's sake rather than because of the people involved

STRENGTHENING ACTIONS THAT PROMOTE AUTONOMY:

Analyzing under what circumstances you want to place your own feelings before the feelings of others

Assuming responsibility for money matters, driving, and repair jobs, instead of expecting the man in your life to handle them

Arranging for shared responsibility of home with family members

Making clear to family members the importance of your work (or schooling) and your need for their cooperation

Pinning down household service persons to a time of arrival

Deciding which responsibilities require perfection and which don't

Increasing an awareness of your own ideas and beliefs as separate from husband, boyfriend, or other prestige figures in your life

Learning methods of handling a physical attack (e.g., rape)

Meeting failure with resistance (rather than passive acceptance)

Developing or maintaining your own interests outside of your family and job

Becoming more of a participant (and less of an observer)

Keeping track of premenstrual tension in order to deal with it more effectively

Initiating introductions (to place you in social control)

Interrupting someone politely when appropriate

STRENGTHENING ACTIONS THAT CONTROL GUILT OR HOSTILITY:

Budgeting time for yourself without feelings of conflict

Facing one day at a time (to keep from being overwhelmed)

Responding firmly but calmly (nonthreateningly) to sexist comments made in ignorance

Coping more effectively with hurt

Viewing failure as a positive factor for growth

Admitting when you are wrong without being self-deprecating

Dissenting without becoming hostile

Recognizing anger and releasing it in deliberate but nonhurtful ways (not denying anger but directing it)

STRENGTHENING ACTIONS FOR RELATING EFFECTIVELY TO OTHERS:

Increasing listening skills

Acknowledging your own needs clearly to yourself and to others

Respecting the "territoriality" of others (your man, your children, your co-workers)

Setting aside regular exclusive togetherness time with significant others (e.g., your man, your child)

Maintaining a sense of responsibility for your children when away at work as well as at home

Familiarizing your family with your place of work (or school) to help them better understand what you do

Handling your own reactions to elderly (and perhaps eccentric) parents (e.g., not overreacting, possibly ignoring)

Being more tolerant of women (or men) who don't have or desire your life style (e.g., homemaker, career woman, volunteer, counter-culture)

Being comfortable with the notion that a woman can earn a large salary and still be feminine

Giving special support to other women as they make changes and go forward with their lives

Developing nonsexual friendships with men

Supporting males in their nonsexist attitudes and dealings with others

Stating how sexist remarks make you feel rather than cutting the person down for saying them (No one can deny what you say you feel.)

STARTER GOALS
FOR STOPPING UNWANTED HABITS

These final lists pertain to habits that the women feel hold them back.

ENDING ACTIONS THAT RESTRICT PERSONAL IDENTITY:

Being "Pollyanna" about life ("fake and pure")

Smiling constantly (the affable front)

Trying to be Superwoman (expecting yourself to do everything and to do it all well)

Reinforcing males who make cracks about your figure, looks, sexiness by the way you respond (coyness, giggling)

Dressing like a sex object while wanting men to admire your mind

Laughing at sexist jokes

Saying "You don't love me or care what happens to me" to get your way

Volunteering to make dessert (salad, main dish) for a dinner party when you are already overcommitted

Dressing to be attractive to others rather than to yourself

Setting yourself apart from other women (e.g., the "Queen Bee" syndrome)

Using "feminine" adjectives in excess ("divine," "lovely," "cute")

Being suggestible

Monopolizing conversations

Exaggerating when reporting an event or telling a story

Talking without listening

Assuming your goals are irrevocable

Overreacting to situations

ENDING ACTIONS THAT RESTRICT SELF-ESTEEM:

Being ingratiating instead of honest

Using "hedges" in sentences (e.g., "*you know*," "*kinda*," "*well*," "*sort of*," "*Do you think you could maybe. . . ?*")*

Using tag words in questions or orders (e.g., "It is difficult, *isn't it?*" "Let's eat now, *shall we?*")†

Excessive apologizing; saying "I'm sorry" repetitively or without real cause

Putting yourself down to yourself or others ("I'm so dumb, such a flake-head")

Withdrawing from frustrating situations (not "sticking it out")

Allowing yourself to be used as a scapegoat (in family matters, sex; by children, friends, spouse)

Using statements full of "shoulds," "musts," and "needs," suggesting absolutist thinking

ENDING ACTIONS THAT RESTRICT AUTONOMY:

Waiting to be given directions before acting

Allowing yourself to be unduly controlled by others' needs

Being reticent to avoid taking a stand

Letting males win rather than trying to do your best

Faking helplessness with men (especially with tears)

Asking others what you should do, rather than planning your own time

Relying on only one person as your source of reinforcement and support

Feeling you must answer any question you're asked, regardless of the circumstances

ENDING ACTIONS THAT RESTRICT CONTROL OF GUILT OR HOSTILITY:

Covering up your negative feelings by overreacting positively

Feeling guilty when you are not doing something "worthwhile"

---

*Robin Lakoff, *Language and Women's Place.* New York: Harpon Colophon, 1975, pp. 53–55.

†Lakoff, *Language and Women's Place,* pp. 14–17.

Declining with many excuses (rather than one or none)

Making anti-male statements or anti-female statements

Assuming male bosses are bastards or female bosses are bitches

Using "killer" labels to make a point or to describe someone ("Male chauvinist!" "You're stupid to think that!" "She's an insensitive clod!")

Being negative: monitoring negatives instead of positives in your life

Blaming others for problems (to avoid taking responsibility for them)

Showing frequent strong emotion when you don't get your way

ENDING ACTIONS THAT RESTRICT RELATING EFFECTIVELY
TO OTHERS:

Asking questions you already know the answer to in order to build up a male ego

Game-playing: flirting with men rather than trying to establish honest communication

"Using" boss/male faculty advisor as substitute father

Excessively questioning others who offer to help ("Do you *really* want to? *Really*? Are you *sure*?")

Allowing people to interrupt you easily with insufficient cause

Subtly manipulating people to do things your way

Giving unsolicited advice

Oversupervising subordinates; stifling their creativity

Pouting, sulking, or brooding when you don't get your way

Complimenting or commenting on superficialities such as clothes, hairdo, makeup

The wording of a goal affects the category it fits. With a starter goal you wish to stop, consider restating it in positive terms ("Become a more active group participant" rather than "Stop being so inactive in groups").

Given what you know now, you will have no problem with your second assignment.

Target Behaviors

CONVERTING STARTER GOALS

To make a starter goal work just for you, simply convert it into even more precise actions that relate to *your own life*. This final pinpointing makes the starter goal relevant just to you and involves real events.

Katie's starter goal is to make up her own mind and stick to it. Because she has learned from childhood to act the docile, passive female, she is easily persuaded to do things she really does not want to (and often later resents). To formulate a target behavior Katie pins down her starter goal (adhering to my own decisions) to the actual situation (not letting Tom talk me into visiting him this weekend when he phones). Katie's target illustrates the specificity needed. It points out *who* (Tom), *when* (tonight when he phones), and *where* (at my apartment). Answers to these questions make the target specific (though sometimes not all are relevant).

Occasions like this occur frequently in Katie's life largely because people know she can be talked into things easily. Therefore she is bound to have chances to select additional target behaviors soon, either with Tom or with someone else.

Here are target behaviors developed by three other women:

STARTER GOAL	TARGET BEHAVIOR
Grace's: Keeping a budget	Next week for the entire week I will keep a record of all money I spend by recording it in a notebook kept in my purse.
Lollie's: Being less of a loner at work	Tomorrow I will eat lunch with the women and men in the front office instead of running errands over the noon hour.
Cara's: Going on a trip by myself	I will drive into Houston alone on Saturday.

Don't assume a target behavior is like a New Year's resolution or an agreement over a handshake. Rather, each target sets the stage for you to apply the psychological principles yet to be discussed.

Many target behaviors spin off one starter goal. However, at first begin your self-change project with a single easy target, proceeding as it is completed to a second and a third of increasing difficulty until your starter goal is accomplished. Maximize your chances for success.

CHOOSING THE BEST TARGET BEHAVIOR

When choosing your target, answer these questions:

Is the target sufficiently small and precise so that it doesn't scare you away? In the target behaviors just mentioned, it is possible for Grace to begin with a goal of less than a week for record-keeping, for Lollie to limit the number of people to lunch with, and for Cara to take a shorter trip alone. A target is not supposed to be overwhelming and difficult but small enough so that while you stretch yourself a little you still have a good chance to complete it successfully.

Is the target one you can practice easily in the near future? Grace, Lollie, and Cara have wisely set their goals within a period of time close at hand. Should she find driving a problem, Cara may prefer to take a bus or train. But she is better off taking the trip over the coming weekend than delaying it unnecessarily.

Is the change one that you yourself want? With women's penchant to please others, remember that your own needs, not boyfriend Homer's or cousin Hildy's, are what count.

The target behaviors you will list on the following chart will be chosen well if you can answer yes to the previous three questions.

Time for Yourself #3

Convert one of your starter goals from Project #2 into three target behaviors. Rank-order the targets according to difficulty and accessibility, placing the easiest one to work on at the top of your list. Target #1 is your first self-change task.

Starter goal:_____

  1. Target:_____

  2. Target:_____

  3. Target:_____

CHAPTER THREE

Woman as Self-Scientist: Objectivity as Eye-Opener

But I don't want to be objective. It hurts my image.

Judy

The real me is standing up and being counted.

Marcy

Systematic, mathematical, objective, analytical: How do these terms strike you? Palatable or unpleasant? On the line below, mark the number that best describes your general feeling about these terms:

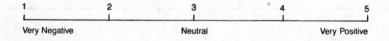

1	2	3	4	5
Very Negative		Neutral		Very Positive

If your rating is above three, you probably already know that your reactions—showing a positive response to things scientific—are different from the stereotypic woman's. If your rating is below three—indicating negative feelings—you probably also know that you are among the countless women who show aversion to the math/science area.

Even with the simplest addition or subtraction of numbers, your aversion could be substantial. Ask yourself who keeps score—a woman or a man—when you play group games, or who is most often the banker when you play Monopoly. Think of the women you know even now who minimize their math/science course work, who shy away from keeping budgets of their own, or who encourage the men in their lives to handle their income tax returns and bank accounts.

No research proves women cannot do well in these areas, even when men may do better. Of course some women possess a stronger ability than others, but since performance is affected adversely by lowered expectations, when we do try we may still feel incompetent, block, stop trying, or even actively withdraw.

Learning the basic tools of self-monitoring is an ideal way to begin to alter these negative notions. Rather than confronting the heady, sophisticated devices of the super-scientist or mathematician, practice easy elementary ways to observe the person you need to know most about—you. The beginnings are so simple you may not realize you have already started by placing an evaluation of your own attitudes on the positive–negative valence scale just discussed.

Advantages of Self-Monitoring

Women, after sorting out facts by monitoring their own actions, come up with significant insights. Consider the following:

COMPARING STEREOTYPIC FEMALE BEHAVIOR TO YOUR OWN

We know which people are dependent, passive, nurturant, and subjective—women, of course. We are also the self-martyring Jewish mother, the submissive Oriental wife, and the strong, assertive black woman. Or the mannish female executive, the unhappy neurotic housewife (especially if we are menopausal), the gracious hostess, the bouncy carefree teenager, the man-hunting college girl, and the overpowering barrel-bosomed committeewoman.

Assumptions result from these stereotypic labels that place expectations on our behavior—sometimes favorable, sometimes unfavorable. Not only do others learn to expect women to act in certain prescribed ways, but we ourselves often assume that we behave in ways attributed to our socialized gender roles when actually we may not.

Take the commonly held notion that women need outsiders' approval for their actions. As a result of monitoring our own behavior, we may find that we do have a high number of approval-seeking reactions, such as asking others' opinions before making most decisions or wanting others to agree with us to justify what we do. Or self-monitoring may show just the opposite: that we have very little need for approval from others and that we are much more independent than we realized. A third possibility is that we look for approval in some kinds of situations (perhaps concerning new projects, buying nonessential items for ourselves, or when seeking independent free time from a husband) but not in others (perhaps selecting children's wardrobes, performing daily functions at our office, or giving a boyfriend a gift). Through the monitoring process we can validate, disconfirm, or qualify female stereotypic actions related to our own lives.

There are two major outcomes. First, we become more aware of starter goals to consider for self-change projects. By observing how we compare with the cultural image—both positive and negative—we recognize ways we would like to be different from the way we are. Take Marian's self-appraisal: "I am much less sensitive to my kids' needs than I realized. I have looked at myself as an earth-mother type, with a cookie jar under my arm, Band-Aids in my apron pocket, and fanny pats proffered at the right moments. But after monitoring my responses to my kids I have to admit that I am much *less* loving in some ways than I thought. I really put my kids down when they don't conform to my expectations, and I want to change this."

Second, we learn we may be further along than we think we are. Sumi, a 29-year-old Japanese–American, shares this: "At times when I thought I was being quiet or permissive I felt self-conscious, because I know women in general and

Japanese women in particular are typecast as passive. I kept thinking I was letting myself conform and felt annoyed I couldn't somehow overcome it. But you know what? I'm much less passive than I thought. After monitoring my own behavior I now realize I'm actually not at all passive when I talk with women friends, or for that matter even with my boss at work. I really feel good about this."

TAKING STOCK OF YOUR OWN ACTIONS

Like a physician who puts the stethoscope to her ears and places the bell-shaped disc from the other end of the tube on her own chest to obtain a measure of her own heartbeat, women tracking their own behaviors can obtain useful measures about their own thoughts, feelings, and ways of reacting. For example, we can detect distortions in our thinking that result from forgetfulness, rationalization, or simply lack of attention. Susan, a sixteen-year-old high schooler says, "I can't believe the mean things I say to my boyfriend, but there they are, staring at me from that paper. I guess I can't ignore them when I've recorded it all myself."

RECOGNIZING YOUR OTHER INFLUENCES

Martha pridefully admits to being seventy-nine years old. She possesses an open mind, a lively curiosity, and wisdom that comes from the perspective of time. "If I had my life to live over," she says, "I'd like to realize early on how much we are influenced by happenstances—little events or situations or people that affect us when we're not aware of it. Even doing what girls were supposed to do I had choices when I didn't realize it. The next time I wouldn't be so much like a leaf on water, floating along without purpose. I'd be more like a boat with a power motor with direction. But I keep working on this, and I'm more in charge now. I've caught up with many of my earlier losses, and I like myself better." The sooner we recognize hidden influences, the sooner we can catch up. Monitoring helps us.

The Eye-Openers:
Personal Data-Collecting Methods

KEEPING JOURNALS OR DIARIES

Probably some time in your life you have kept your own journals or diaries. They are the most common forms of personal record-keeping, but their effectiveness as tools to increase self-direction varies greatly. A narrative account merely mentioning events, a sort of written calendar, is rarely helpful.

Diaries and journals reflecting one's own attitudes are better. Well-known feminist and diarist Anais Nin became expert at exploring her own feelings in this way, and her records are not only valuable sources of personal information but insightful contributions to women's literature.

In self-change, monitoring does not require a writer's talents to describe or embellish, but it does require clear reporting of actions and feelings.

KEEPING LOGS

For our purposes, logs are an improvement over journals and diaries because logs help systematize our thinking and actions.

Sarah, whose closed-circuit TV sales work entails flying to visit clients in several states, keeps track of ideas for possible starter goals in a small notebook she tucks in her purse. In it she records starter goal possibilities when they first occur to her, regardless of whether she is on a plane, waiting for a client, or in her own apartment. The risk of forgetting or distorting by recording later is thus minimized.

Tracking specific target options is another reason to log new ideas. Ellen describes herself as shy. One of her starter goals is to express her feelings more openly. Since she thinks only certain occasions are appropriate, she decides to keep track of day-to-day possibilities first, then later decide where she wants to start. She devised a log sheet that begins like this:

42

STARTER GOAL: EXPRESSING FEELINGS MORE OPENLY

Date	Possible Target Behavior
2/9	Being clear with refrigerator repair person about specific morning to come over so that I don't hold more time open to get the job done.
2/12	Explaining to Brian that it makes me uncomfortable when he doesn't consult me before accepting a party invitation for both of us.
2/13	Telling Dad that Saturdays are a bad time for me to visit and arrange another time that is convenient for both of us.
2/16	Suggesting at work that I would like to have the mail run on Tuesdays to coincide with my afternoon meetings.
2/16	Explaining to Jerry that I need advance notice to drive him to swim team and why it upsets other plans if he asks me at the last minute.

Ellen's log-keeping helps point up justifiable occasions for telling others how she feels. Even given her shyness, she is now more motivated to choose a specific target to work on in the near future because she has a list to start from.

Logging is also useful for learning the self-change skills in the chapters ahead. Here, for example, is a section of Jacky's log from a self-change project on giving more honest positive feedback to others. Note that her log includes a list for others' reactions.

STARTER GOAL: GIVING HONEST POSITIVE FEEDBACK

Date	My Action	Reactions from Others
6/8	I told Jim how much I appreciated his waiting for me.	He seemed pleased. Squeezed my hand.
6/9	I mentioned to Mrs. Allen how much her letter meant to us when we knew she was terribly busy.	She smiled.
6/9	When Eve dropped by I told her how the support she had given my suggestion had helped with the vote.	She told me that she would really like to work on more projects with me because we seemed to agree on many things.

Date	My Action	Reactions from Others
6/10	Mom called. I mentioned how thankful I was that she was able to postpone her visit until a more convenient time.	She said she genuinely hoped I could always tell her if the time was inconvenient. I feel good about our relationship.

In this log Jacky not only notes her own progress but others' reactions—mainly positive—and these strengthen her desire to continue.

In the next two chapters you will see how logging can also increase your knowledge about your own personal pleasures and the ways you react to fear or stress.

COUNTING RESPONSES

Carefully keeping track of ways you react gives you ideas about your performance that are more accurate than your own hunches.

Let's look at a fictitious set of parents. Barbara and Bob, both of whom have office jobs, disagree on who most often responds during the night when their small children need them. By placing tally marks on a sheet of paper taped to the bathroom wall, they easily determine after a two-week period that Bob does indeed get up more often with the children than Barbara.

Surprised, Barbara wants to try a second method of record-keeping—to count not only the number of times they each get up but to record the length of time as well. After keeping track several more weeks, they find that during that period Barbara is the one who loses the most sleep because of the duration of time she stays up with the children. On one occasion Bob calls her to change a bed and on another a sick child asks for her even though Bob is the first person up.

Any limited-time sample can easily distort a situation, and judgment is necessary with such simple recording to take this into account. Our main interest here is to contrast two counting methods.

Recording either *frequency* of responses or *duration* of responses will measure your performance level. It is up to you to decide which way to count. Here are some examples of responses women have kept track of:

FREQUENCY

How often I apologize about my apartment not being clean

How often I make "killer" (super-strong, often hurtful) statements to get my point across

How often I feel guilty when I'm not doing something "useful"

How often I *really* relinquish control over housework chores when someone else performs them

How often I pick up conversational cues from others

DURATION

Length of time I spend playing with my kids

Length of time I spend talking on the phone

Length of time I listen without interrupting

Length of time it takes me to wind up a conversation

Length of time I spend talking about pleasant, noncomplaining topics to husband (boyfriend)

Simple imaginative devices help us count our responses. Wrist or golf-score counters are available (in most sports departments or golf shops). We can keep a pencil and a 3 × 5 card in a purse for tallying. When it's difficult to write, try a sheet of paper from which bits can be torn off after each response and later counted, or keep track by moving pennies or toothpicks from one sweater (or purse) pocket to another. All of these measure frequency of responses.

Duration is more difficult to measure. Sometimes stopwatches are used, and on occasion other people are corralled to observe and time a person's actions. (Today inexpensive quartz watches often have timers.) Occasionally, a precise measurement isn't needed: "Look, Chris, I know I have this habit of arguing when I'm on the defensive. You're around me a lot. Help me keep track. See if I'm cutting down at all."

RATING FEELINGS

Sometimes people benefit by knowing how strong or how weak their feelings really are. To obtain a measure of the intensity of our feelings we can devise a simple rating scale with numerical values. Usually segments up to five are sufficient to represent both positive and negative values, such as those illustrated at the beginning of this chapter, but scales can range to nine or even higher if we want more refined differences. The basic idea is to obtain our subjective measure of the intensity of a given feeling—happiness, eagerness, satisfaction, anger, frustration, depression, jealousy, guilt, or whatever. At the same time we can note the various conditions under which a feeling is strong or weak.

Jane complains of being depressed yet finds herself unable to describe what makes her feel that way. (This is often true of women who feel blue, because the feeling can be so pervasive that at first it is hard to sort out what contributes to the problem.) With some assistance from an outsider, Jane compiles a five-point scale and begins a self-observation project:

1 = Very happy; feeling great about life
2 = Moderately happy; above average good feelings
3 = Neutral; no strong feelings either way
4 = Moderately depressed; unhappy but sticking it out
5 = Very depressed; hard to keep going at all

During a two-week period she rates her mood changes. By keeping track of her feelings she becomes much more aware of the conditions that accompany her depression and even notes certain cyclical tendencies in her moods, which she can then anticipate and deal with in advance. Here is a sample day's ratings:

Date	Rating	Activity
8/6	4	Getting up in morning
	3	Meeting with Bobby's teacher
	3	Grocery shopping
	5	Picking up house (I can't get myself to do this)
	4	Watching daytime soap opera
	4	Cooking dinner
	4	Cleaning up after dinner
	2	Talking with Bill in the evening

After ten days of monitoring activities that affect her depression level, Jane is able to set up starter goals that increase some of the activities associated with lowering her depression level (spending more time with adults on a one-to-one basis, arranging more activities away from home during the day) and decrease time spent on activities tending to raise it (requesting more family cooperation to keep the house from being littered, assigning jobs to children at mealtime).

Depression among women is not uncommon during the middle years. Increasing positive or neutral experiences while decreasing negative ones can help reduce it. Sometimes women do this themselves by working on starter goals to boost their morale (playing tennis, changing jobs, caring for a pet, meeting more people). If the depression is severe, women will want to seek trained professional help for support. Depression can usually be cured. Why suffer needlessly?

Some women note an increase in moodiness prior to their menstrual periods. If this is true for you, this valuable information can help you anticipate and handle the predictable "down" period through actions planned in advance. Starter goals to help counteract premenstrual depression include exercising before the onset of cramps or when depression is first noticed, planning to take in a movie or cultural event with a friend to keep your mind off moodiness and not "pass it around," deliberately employing self-statements such as "This is only temporary. Be patient," or "Lucky me. I'm not pregnant." For severe premenstrual stress, don't hesitate to seek professional assistance.

KEEPING STRUCTURED DIARIES

Designed specifically to help recognize situational influences surrounding our actions, the structured diary is a good way to understand our own circumstances better. These are its categories:

Date	Introductory Factors (Antecedents)	Behavior	Resulting Factors (Consequences)
	Factors that preceded or were present when behavior was enacted. When did it happen, with whom, where, what were you doing?	Action or feeling being monitored (starter goal or target behavior)	Results of behavior: Were they pleasant or unpleasant? Describe what happened.

Christine's starter goal is to reduce arguments with her husband, so she decides to keep a structured diary to monitor surrounding influences that possibly contribute to their problem. The entries that follow are abstracted from a longer list.

Date	Introductory Factors	Behavior	Resulting Factors
10/10	Over cocktails before dinner	Argument with Jack over when to take trip.	I was upset, gloomy, Jack read paper.
10/13	Over drinks before dinner. Jack tired. Dinner late.	Argument over whether to buy new drapes.	Dinner burned.

Date	Introductory Factors	Behavior	Resulting Factors
10/17	Cocktails before dinner.	Argument over who should discipline Mike (son) for getting in late.	Both of us got angry, difficult to talk.
10/18	Cocktails on porch	Continued argument about Mike.	Didn't eat much for dinner.
10/20	Jack fell asleep while I was talking to him. Before-dinner drinks.	Argument about Jack not listening.	Felt guilty about blowing my stack.

Looking over Christine's structured diary, we quickly arrive at the same conclusion she does; namely, that for them the cocktail hour is a poor time to discuss family problems—perhaps because she and her husband need to relax from their day's work or because their drinking lessens the usual controls over their actions. In any event, they decide to limit their before-dinner drinking and to confine discussions to pleasant events of the day. They agree to settle family issues after eating. Recognizing situational factors helps them focus on ways to curb the disruptive sessions and possibly to eliminate the need for marital counseling.

Analyzing the results of a given action often helps us understand why it continues. The starter goal for Erin, a junior college freshman, is to stop acting helpless, because she realizes this tendency creates dependency upon others. She decides to keep a structured diary about those occasions when she displays helplessness. Listed below are three of her entries:

Date	Introductory Factors	Behavior	Resulting Factors
3/7	Gary, after school.	Told Gary I could not get my car started.	Gary started car. (It was flooded.) We drove to get a milkshake.
3/10	Dad, after supper, at home.	I yelled for him because there was a big moth in my room and I didn't want to hurt it.	Dad released it outside and gave me a hug, saying, "You're still my little girl."

Date	Introductory Factors	Behavior	Resulting Factors
3/11	Mary, before chemistry tests.	Phoned Mary about chemistry quiz. Me: "I don't get any of it. I'll flunk."	Mary spent 45 minutes explaining sample test items to me.

Looking over her structured diary, Erin realizes that one of her problems is that she not only "gets by" with obtaining help unnecessarily from others, but that she often is actually rewarded for it (the milkshake, the hug, the answers to review questions). She knows she needs somehow to arrange her life so that it will not be so easy to receive pleasurable outcomes when she relies on others. One young woman working on a similar problem told those people whom she was most likely to lean on not to give in to her, thereby cueing them to different behavior that would encourage less dependency.

Following are other personal actions women have chosen to scrutinize with structured diaries in order to uncover surrounding influences:

Speaking out quickly to avoid silences in conversations
Putting down my own ability in front of others
Putting others down
Allowing myself to be "walked on"
Waiting to be given directions before acting
Interrupting when someone else is talking
Making anti-female statements
Making anti-male statements

Time for Yourself #5

Select an action of your own you would like to examine, one you can observe frequently over a period of a week or so. Each time the action occurs, note immediately (or as soon as possible) the surrounding introductory and resulting factors. What insights do you find that might influence your behavior in the future?

Date	Introductory Factors	Behavior	Resulting Factors

CHARTING PROGRESS

So far we have centered on how to understand our own actions better through self-observation. Charting personal progress is a natural extension. To do this, simply make a histogram indicating the number of your responses (frequency or duration) on the vertical axis and the time interval you select on the horizontal axis. The time interval is most likely to be daily, but it may be shorter (hourly) or longer (weekly), depending on what is measured.

The purpose of the chart is to give us graphic data about our responses during two separate but connected time periods. These periods are called baseline and intervention periods. (See Lisa's graph.) During the baseline periods we monitor our current actions, making no attempt to change them. During the intervention periods we *try* to change (applying methods we will soon address) and monitor the results.

Feedback is important for self-change. We need to know how we're doing, and with a graph we see before-and-after comparisons that help us judge whether our change strategies are working. Then we are spurred on if we are improving or are able to analyze what's wrong if we're not.

Take Lisa as an example. She is a supervisor in the credit division of a bank. Her graph is based on her starter goal; namely, giving orders to others in the form of statements

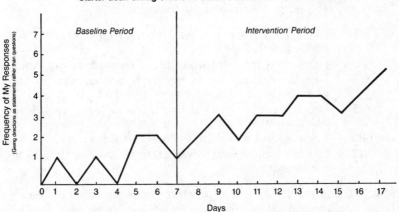

Starter Goal: Giving Orders as Statements Rather Than as Questions

rather than questions. (Example: "Please bring the folder to me," not "Do you think it would be a good idea to bring the folder for me to look at?") The graph shows both her baseline and intervention periods.

The effectiveness of Lisa's intervention methods is illustrated in the graph by increased frequency in giving orders as statements. Notice that her baseline period produces a slight elevation of responses even though she has not started intervention. A common occurrence, this happens because of a person's increased attention on the act during the baseline period.

Lisa's goal is clearly worded, and this helps her know exactly what responses to tally. She might have chosen instead to chart the action she wants to stop; namely, her habit of giving orders as tentative questions. In that case her baseline would show higher rather than lower frequency at the start. But eventually she needs to increase desirable responses, and stating her goal positively helps to start this right away.

LOGGING BASELINE AND INTERVENTION

An alternative to the graph is to keep track of baseline and intervention periods simply by maintaining written descriptions of relevant actions. Michele says her tendency to overreact is causing problems with her boyfriend, Steve, so her starter goal is to reduce this tendency especially in situations with him (where they are most likely to occur). During several days of "baseline," she logs the following overreactions:

8/30   I kept talking about what a poor game of tennis I was playing (with Steve).

9/2   I screamed too loud when Steve stepped on my foot.

9/3   I spilled strawberries on my pants and got really upset when Steve and I were eating breakfast.

9/5   I raged when another driver failed to signal as I drove Steve to work.

9/6   I overreacted when Steve dozed off during sex.

9/7   I jumped and shook when Steve dropped a jar into an empty wastebasket.

Now quite conscious of her current actions, Michele easily starts intervention. Here are excerpts taken from her log:

9/9   I didn't run away from an angry situation with Steve. I stayed and dealt with it.

9/10   Steve stepped on my toe. I remembered in time and plastered a smile on my face while pointing to my foot. He saw what had happened and we both laughed.

9/12   Steve stepped on my "in basket" which was on the floor. No damage was done and I remained calm.

9/13   Steve squeezed my knee in a way that drives me up the wall. Instead of crying out, I took his hand away, and that gesture was enough to remind him of how it bothered me.

9/15   Same situation as 9/13
Later, same evening: Steve was rubbing my leg from thigh to near the knee, and I pointed out that I liked that a lot. (It sure beats knee-squeezing.)

Michele describes her new behavior as calmer and more controlled, stating that she now usually thinks first before she reacts. She adds, "After recording my baseline, I have become so conscious of this problem that I find myself stopping overreactions to *other* situations where Steve is not even involved, though occasionally I do still slip." Michele will continue to work on this change. Her motivation remains high, first because her baseline makes her overreactive behavior more obvious to her, and second because Steve is glad to assist.

Self-scientists keep an open mind. Promise yourself not to dilute what you do with a half-hearted approach.

CHAPTER FOUR

In Pursuit of Purely Personal Pleasures

What pleases me most is seeing others happy.
Great-Grandma Victoria

Sometimes I wonder if I enjoy feeling guilty.
Charlotte

Try this. Check the clock and for one minute write down as many pleasures, gratifications, and rewarding activities for yourself as you can. Next, think of someone close to you and for another minute write down as many as possible for that person. Now count the items on each list. Are you a woman who recalls more pleasurable activities for a significant other person than for yourself? Men performing this exercise frequently make longer lists of their own pleasures than women do. Do the men in your life have an edge on you when it comes to knowing what they enjoy?

If your answer is yes to either of these questions, don't feel you are unjustly singled out, because many of us still need reminders to rejoice in our own pleasures as well as to rejoice in the pleasures of those we love. Read on for the reasons why this is so important.

TO BALANCE YOUR OWN NEEDS
WITH THE NEEDS OF OTHERS

Bess takes part in a transitional women's workshop. Her comments: "I loved sharing my daughter's sense of accomplishment recently when she brought home her first real paycheck, and again the other day when my son took a girl to the movies after agonizing over whether she would go with him. Of course, any time my husband receives some plaudit at work I feel very proud. These are *my* gratifications, not just theirs. But emphasizing my *own* personal pleasures? I have a hard time with that. I *prefer* being an important part of someone else's life."

Because of habits long formed, women like Bess have trouble acknowledging or even identifying pleasures strictly their own. Without this balance, guilt undermines occasions to value themselves that otherwise could be turned into real sources of joy and opportunities for personal growth.

TO EXPERIENCE A SENSE
OF ACCOMPLISHMENT

At age 56 Rose, disenchanted with her traditional role as homemaker, takes a week to monitor personal pleasures in her daily routine. Expecting to find few, she discovers instead that she actually gains many enjoyments from the life she leads (baking special breads, experimenting with gourmet recipes, planning parties, volunteering at the Red Cross, serving on a church board). There are extensions of her daily activities that she wants to work on, but her career as a homemaker now gives her a sense of well-being and usefulness she did not have before.

The possibility of deriving more personal satisfactions from everyday events surfaces when we monitor and thereby focus our attention either on sizable activities such as Rose's, or on small incidental accomplishments and improvements such as these contributed by other women:

Arranging things so my four-year-old daughter doesn't heckle me when visitors come

Being told I act like my mom

Remaining in control when shopping for shoes (I'm hard to fit and salespeople give me a hard time)

Being accepted as a fellow student by younger students

Completing my jogging

Being confided in by someone I like

Knowing the volunteer committee I'm on is functioning well

Feeling I have really made a difference in the life of a hospital patient I talk to

Understanding how the library works

Realizing how efficiently I have learned to grocery-shop

Recognizing I can now be happy when I am alone (I am recently divorced)

Feeling confident because I organized tonight's company dinner before I went to work today

Not using my headache as an excuse for being late to work

Gratifications like these go a long way toward helping women feel better about themselves, but only provided they are valued as positive achievements. *They need to be hailed, not hidden.* It's a "Look, Ma, I did it!" attitude. So instead of merely accepting her accomplishment of putting the children to bed on time, Marty responds thoroughly and positively to this fact, deliberately taking five minutes to flop into the easy chair and say to herself, "How great! I got the kids to bed on time. Fait accompli! I deserve a little extra time right now just to enjoy the silence. Ahhh! Lovely!"

One woman expressed it this way: "I remember once telling my mother-in-law that she was the only person I felt free to brag to about my husband's successes. Now I've decided that *I'm* the best possible person to brag to about my own. I've learned to dangle my previously little-noticed accomplishments before my own eyes, and it works. Impressing myself this way *does* help raise my confidence level."

TO HELP WITH SELF-CHANGE

Knowing what pleases us is essential for the success of self-change. This alone is an important reason to recognize what makes us feel good. In future chapters we will select certain gratifications to use under carefully arranged conditions to be described. Together they will help us change our own behavior.

Pleasure Sources

Samples of other women's gratifications follow, to suggest the far-ranging possibilities of your own pleasures. What others occur to you?

SPORTS

Athletics, an interest area that carries social reward value as well as health benefits, is also an antidepressant. Here women include: bike riding, swimming, jogging, playing volleyball, playing tennis or racquetball, walking or hiking, ice skating or roller skating, horseback riding, using a punching bag, modern dancing, playing Frisbee, rowing on a crew, skiing, aerobic dancing, and climbing trees.

CREATIVE ACTIVITIES

Women have a long history of skills in this area. Some of these are now being revitalized and expanded: knitting a sweater or mittens, stitchery or needlepoint, framing a picture, quilting, sewing a dress or skirt, weaving, baking bread, preparing a favorite meal (coq au vin, squash casserole), gardening, listening to music, playing the piano or guitar, building a hi fi set, polishing jewelry, playing chess, participating in a play, taking part in an art exhibit, outlining a paper, refinishing a table, building a playhouse, oil painting, writing poetry or fiction, interior decorating, and arranging flowers.

PERSONAL SHOPPING

When it comes to shopping for pleasurable items for ourselves, many women feel guilty. As a full-time homemaker Ellen knows that her housework and child care deserve compensation, but since she does not receive a paycheck, she has great

difficulty buying anything for herself. Her solution is to establish a kitty and pay herself the minimum wage for hourly
work she performs beyond an eight-hour day. She reasons
that she then has guilt-free mad money unrelated to living
expenses, and quite a bit it is, despite her modest compensation.

Here are sample pleasure items taken from some women's
personal shopping lists: new record album, antique flower vase,
new plant, fresh flowers, pocket calculator, extra roll of film,
Halloween mask, new blouse, crazy wind-up toy, special wrap-
ping paper, cosmetics (new color mascara, fake fingernails),
black stockings, and cloisonné earrings.

Along with shopping for something specific, some women
find pleasure collecting ideas by window shopping, or from bar-
gain-hunting at flea markets, antique shops, or garage sales.

Think back on how you have spent your free time and mad
money in the past. It will help you clarify what kinds of shopping
you do for purely personal pleasure.

FOOD

High on the lists of gratification sources are eating and drinking. Overindulgence is a weighty problem, but food is nevertheless a potentially powerful gratifier and one that is
accessible. As a special treat, may it serve you well! Here are
some women's tastes: wonton soup, home-baked dark bread,
Columbian coffee, buttermilk pancakes, jelly beans, manicotti,
big juicy apple, angel cake with chocolate frosting, butter-
scotch milkshake, artichokes, fresh picked tender raw pole
beans, cold glass of beer, and truffles.

PEOPLE

This category tops almost everyone's list, especially when it
pertains to approval from others (a parent, friend, spouse,
child, or even a stranger). Also mentioned: having friends drop
by, phoning one's family, good conversation, writing a loved
one, staying with a boyfriend, getting mail, lunching with the
gang, campaigning for a political candidate, taking a study

break with a roommate, talking over the day's activities, and going on a trip with someone special.

Notice that this list does not include many vital pleasures associated with affection such as fondling, making love, and hugging. Affection itself is such a constant in any good relationship between people that it surely is a major source of gratification, but it can be abused and misused. We will discuss how in Chapter six.

RELAXATION

Generally when we think of relaxation we first think of play. But relaxation is also a simple release of tension. Crying, for instance, can be both beneficial and relaxing, and since for women it is also permissible, this surely is a cultural advantage we have over men. Others: a hot bath or shower, sitting around a fire, seeing a good movie or watching TV, sleeping late, playing cards, reading a good novel or a favorite magazine, playing with or walking the dog, sleeping between fresh sheets, doing "nothing," running barefoot in cool grass, yoga, browsing in bookstores, lying on the ground watching the clouds roll by, cooking dinner, having a massage, jogging, watching a sunset, taking a nap, and setting the table artistically for company.

OTHER ENJOYABLE HABITS

Even if we think our daily lives are filled with drudgery or boredom, certain pleasures sometimes develop from habit. Ask yourself, "What in my everyday life would I hate to give up?" Here are some answers from other women: drinking ice water, discussing current events, polishing silver, driving home from work alone, blow-drying my hair, looking through grandma's attic, taking coffee breaks at the office, sitting in the garden, putting on makeup, washing the car, eating crunchy granola for breakfast, winning "when it's all luck," winning (unqualified), and reading the paper after dinner.

Negative Gratifications

Certain gratifications are harmful. Watch out for these.

SELF–PITY

Terry, stuck at home because her child has the flu, phones her aunt. She describes her loneliness, what plans have been disrupted, how long she waited to see the pediatrician, how difficult it is to keep the child in bed. "You poor thing. It must be very hard," her aunt responds when Terry eventually stops talking. "I just wish I could help. Get a sitter and have lunch with me tomorrow. It will give you a change."

Terry next phones an acquaintance, then a neighbor. They all commiserate with her. Even the mailwoman has an earful. Her self-pity really pays off.

We all deserve a chance to "bitch" once in a while. Airing one's feelings is justifiable, even healthy. But if we continually seek opportunities to talk about our troubles in order to gain attention and sympathy from others, we are indulging in self-pity.

SELF–PUNISHMENT

Negative or ambivalent messages that women receive in our society easily foster feelings of inadequacy. These, or any other "confirmations" of low self-opinions that we may already hold, are gratifying when they serve to validate what we already think of ourselves. Put another way, if we don't like ourselves much, for whatever reasons, self-punishment may not only be reasonable but pleasurable.

We don't refer here to severe self-destruction such as mutilation and suicide—these are problems for professionals. Rather we discuss subtle forms of self-abuse that we *can* cope with such as verbal self-put-downs, disregard for the care of our bodies, exploitive self-exposure to criticism from others or not allowing ourselves the same pleasures we encourage others to follow. These promote self-disrespect.

Excellent starter goals are available if you discover punishing gratifications that you want to stop. Here are a few that other women have worked on: increasing the number of positive statements I give myself, regularly eating a nutritious balance of food, making a point of staying away from my sister when she is super-critical, saving Tuesday afternoons for myself. Notice how these starter goals help counter each of the low self-opinions mentioned in the previous paragraph.

OVERINDULGENCE

Overindulgence, another source of harmful pleasure, can also be a form of self-punishment. The possible gratifications we receive from eating or refusing to eat, smoking, drug abuse (including alcohol), shopping, sleeping late, daydreaming, or other habits with potentially harmful excesses all need our monitoring to prevent abuse. The high incidence of alcoholism and anorexia (excessive dieting) among women, for example, is well documented. If you recognize overindulgence as your problem, try applying self-change techniques. If you find you are unable to use behavior-change methods without help, don't hesitate to seek professional assistance. Learning how to control your own indulgences can change your life.

UNLAWFUL BEHAVIOR

To the person who has not been caught, breaking the law can be a source of satisfaction. The shoplifter is gratified by successfully obtaining a wanted object, yet not having to pay for it. Each time a shoplifter is not caught, the chance is greater that she or he will try again. After a number of successes, even being caught once is not always a strong deterrent. Statistics on shoplifting show that many more women than men are guilty of this misdemeanor. The incidence of women robbing banks has also greatly increased. Gratification from being successful at taking certain kinds of risks encourages criminal activity.

HURTING OTHERS

Janice claims, "I get a kick out of teasing my boyfriend when he misspells words. He is a terrible speller and he knows it.

He just laughs when I kid him about it so I love to tease him."

How does that old song go? "Laughing on the outside, crying on the inside?"* Teasing is almost always uncomfortable if not painful to the person who is the brunt of it. Even if *you* may find it pleasurable, it is risky and not a gratification we recommend.

Hurting others is sometimes justified by disclaimers such as "just getting even," "only proving my point," "he/she deserved it." All of this may be true, but let's not make use of this form of personal gratification for our purposes here.

If you think some of your pleasures are really camouflaged negative gratifications, think of starter goals to help you change.

Pleasures are as individual as a person's life style. Our job is to become more and more aware of what these gratifications are in our own lives. Monitoring your own actions and sharing your gratification ideas with others will pay off in self-understanding.

Time for Yourself #6

For one week, keep a list of all the varied pleasurable experiences that occur in your life each day. At the end of that time, formulate groupings centered around the gratification categories in this chapter. Examine your own findings in view of what you have just read.

---

*From a song by that title written by Ben Raleigh and Bernie Wayne, © 1946, Broadcast Music, Inc.

CHAPTER FIVE

Controlling the Panic Buttons

> On days when I'm really tense I feel like a stiff cardboard box sealed with fiber tape and tied with taut string. Somewhere inside, packed with cotton, there must surely be a relaxed, comfortable somebody called Becky.
>
> Becky

> The more I face up to what scares me, the larger my world becomes.
>
> Adrienne

When we talk about panic buttons, we refer to stress reactions we all experience that are activated by everyday occurrences. We associate them with discomfort, tension, guilt, worry, helplessness, and especially fear. For our purposes here we do not include debilitating or phobic reactions.

Women and men in our society react differently to fear. It isn't that men don't initially have fears or that they cease being afraid, but generally they are forced either to face them or to conceal them. Women, however, often are not expected to face their fears or conceal them either. In fact, we are encouraged to retain our fears by being taken care of. In this

63

tradition men often still say protectively, "Let me enter first," help a woman across a busy street, or get up at night to check on a noise in the kitchen.

Women are often laughed at or teased when they show fear. That makes the phrase "weaker sex" take on substantiated meaning. Some women accept this inference of weakness, internalize it, and look upon themselves as inept.

Sources of Fear

CULTURAL MESSAGES

Fears are often so much a part of women's existence that they are woven into the fabric of our lives. They exist for several reasons, but one major source is paramount—our socialization. Check over the starter goal examples of fear and stress listed by women in Chapter two and you will understand how many socialized fears inhibit us from enlarging our personal worlds.

OTHER PEOPLE'S EXPECTATIONS

Closely allied to our own cultural messages are other peoples' notions regarding *our* behavior. Trudi, because of family training, is under tension to make high grades. Camille frets when her hair is cut shorter than her boyfriend likes it. Carol is apprehensive because people say she can't be a good mother if she also works full-time. And Leslie, who has several fastidious women friends, finds herself dusting her apartment more often for fear her housekeeping is not up to *their* standards.

ASSOCIATION WITH UNPLEASANTNESS

Not least, we become fearful because we associate a present situation with one that previously caused us pain or punishment.

> PAULA: Men? No way. I'm off them entirely after what Larry did to me.

64

AMY: I can't face driving in city traffic after that accident.

DEIRDRE: I've learned to shut up in class. People tease me about being a brain. I don't mind it as much from the girls, but when guys do it, I'm terribly embarrassed.

These women do not want to expose themselves to more misery even if it means constricting their lives.

Though it may be helpful to know the origins of our fears, it is usually not essential to know *why* they exist in order to do something about them. Remember that what is learned can usually be unlearned. These panic buttons—whether a result of our culture, of others' expectations of us, of imitating the behavior of others, or of associations with former unpleasant experiences—can usually be controlled and overcome.

Recognizing Your Distress Signals

SYMPTOMS

You may think that you are aware of your own tension. But remember for a moment the last time you really blew up about something. Can you describe how your mind responded, whether your stomach reacted, if your palms were sweaty, when your breathing began to quicken? Under stress our composite reaction is usually so blurred by the stress itself that we don't recognize symptoms until they escalate sharply. By then it is more difficult or even impossible to control our feelings and easy to panic completely.

But this can be changed. If we sharpen the detection of our tension, the early symptoms themselves can become signals for quick counteraction before things really get out of hand. Women who kept track of their own signs of tension over a period of time were asked to divide the symptoms arbitrarily into either physical or social categories. Here are some of their responses. Ask yourself which of these symptoms are ones you experience yourself and note others they remind you of.

CATHY

by Cathy Guisewite

TO REDUCE STRESS, RECOGNIZE SYMPTOMS *BEFORE* THEY ESCALATE

PHYSICAL SYMPTOM

> Antsy stomach, "pregnant" knot in stomach, nausea, growling stomach, diarrhea, inability to eat, lump in throat, dry mouth
>
> Overall perspiration, feeling hot, sweaty palms, cold hands, goose-bumps
>
> Increased pulse and heartbeat

Sighing, holding breath, quickening breath, shallow breathing, crying

Knuckle-cracking, foot-tapping, knee-jerking, nail-biting, pacing, lip-biting, inability to sit still

Using hands: twiddling thumbs, finger-tapping, hair-twisting

Tiredness, yawning, falling asleep, wakefulness during night

Headache, backache, body-shaking, teeth-grinding or jaw-clenching, facial twinges

Trembling voice, change in voice pitch (high or low), need to clear throat, swallowing or inability to swallow

Need to urinate frequently

SOCIAL SYMPTOMS

Shyness, withdrawal, silence, loneliness, fright

Depression

Helplessness

Mental blocking: memory loss, inability to listen, hesitancy of speech, stuttering

Awkwardness: difficulty in acting natural or in laughing easily, consciousness of hands and body posture, averting eyes

Talkativeness, fake or uncontrollable laughter, giggling, repetitive speech ("you know," "okay," "gross," "shit")

Increased smoking, use of drugs

Increased or decreased eating

Impatience, "sharpness," being "hyper"

Utter calm, inability to act

Snobbishness, acting "distant," sarcasm

Sudden accident-proneness

These symptoms may be clues to other issues besides fear. But when several appear together, chances are they are tension-related.

We each respond to stress in our own ways. Since we are often unaware of our tension symptoms unless we deliberately look for them, glance over the lists once again. They will help you devise a list of your own.

TENSION LEVEL

When you are familiar with your own symptoms, you are ready to judge how tense you feel at any given time. The method to be described not only increases awareness of your own tensions, but also marks their fluctuations, helping you understand variations in your stress level.

The Subjective Units of Discomfort Scale* helps people assess how uncomfortable they are at any given time. It is a self-measurement device based upon each person's subjective evaluation of her or his anxiety level. Women using this simple technique find it a way of acknowledging to themselves and sometimes even communicating to others the degree of discomfort or tension they feel at a given time. The measurement is called a *SUDS* level, *SUDS* being the acronym for Subjective Units of Discomfort Scale.

Here is the way you determine your own *SUDS* level. Imagine a scale from zero to 100 in which zero represents the most relaxing and pleasant state you can think of. To describe their lowest imagined *SUDS* level, some women mention the period immediately following sex, when tranquillity and total relaxation prevail. Another woman describes a panoramic beach scene in which she sits alone on a hot day letting cool sand ooze between her toes, listening to the rhythmic breaking of the waves and smelling clean, fresh salt water. She says she wants a few people around for safety, "but not close. And no beach buggies." Note how many senses this woman incorporates into her imagined state. Fantasize to yourself what your own zero *SUDS* experience might be.

*J. Wolpe and A. Lazarus, *Behavior Therapy Techniques.* New York: Pergamon Press, 1966, p. 73.

Now turn to the opposite end of the scale. One hundred on your *SUDS* is represented by feelings of total panic, of frozen fear. Imagining being held down and raped is most frequently mentioned. The thought of looking out of an airplane window and seeing an engine drop off stirs strong reactions. A woman who does not swim envisions her peak *SUDS* level as falling out of a boat into icy water and high waves. Another with a fear of closed places imagines being stuck in an elevator full of people. What would 100 on your own *SUDS* be?

Say that a rating of 50 is the average level of tension, day in and day out, for most people. Dorie places her average *SUDS* level at 77. "I don't think I show it openly, but I am a pretty tense person. I always have to be doing something even when I'm supposed to be relaxing. One time I made the mistake of arranging a week's vacation on an island with nothing to do, and I nearly died. If I didn't have something to worry about I would think something *was* wrong!" On the other hand Diane, placid and contemplative, reveals she was once told by a male friend that if someone tiptoed up behind her and said, "Gotcha!" she probably wouldn't even jump. Diane decided to rate her average *SUDS* level at 21.

Ask yourself what your own average *SUDS* level is: 24? 30? 55? 81?

With the extreme ends of your scale established, and with an idea about *your* average *SUDS* level, you can now obtain comparisons between your own reactions in various situations. Samantha is a woman who has kept track of her *SUDS* level by logging it, and she shares a day from her record:

Date	SUDS Level	Situation
4/5	20	Hot shower upon rising.
	69	Smeared makeup. Out of time. Big rush.
	75	Ran to catch bus. Out of breath.
	40	At desk on time. Relief. Time to recoup.
	80	Boss asked me to redo paper. Big job.
	68	Todd phoned me at office. Hard to talk.
	30	Window-shopped over lunch. Time for myself.

Date	SUDS Level	Situation
	35	Talked with S., P., & T. at water cooler.
	74	Boss on intercom. Wanted paper, still unfinished.
	55	Placed completed paper on her desk.
	20	Sauna in apt. building.
		Phone call to Mom:
	27	—wrote down her chicken recipe
	70	—Mom: "Why don't you come home oftener?"

By becoming aware of her fluctuating *SUDS* level Samantha has a tool that helps measure her tension under a variety of conditions. Try measuring yours.

Time for Yourself #8

Keep track of fluctuations in your *SUDS* level for three days, noting particularly the peaks and dips. Record the situations that triggered the variations.

Date   *SUDS Level*   *Situation*

As you become more aware of tension levels, you will notice times when in comparison to others you retain control quite well. Sarah, a former elementary school teacher with small children of her own, is surprised to find two of her friends reporting highly elevated *SUDS* levels when disciplining other people's children. *Sarah:* "I didn't realize disciplining others' kids was such a strain on mothers. It doesn't bother me at all. I guess having been a teacher really pays off here." Other potentially stressful circumstances individual women note they can handle:

Comforting a dying person
Answering weird phone calls
Staying alone at night
Accepting criticism without defensiveness

Working for a much younger person
Initiating a relationship with a man
Catching and reporting errors when overcharged at a store
Changing a flat tire
Fixing an overflowing toilet
Attending a movie alone
Traveling alone in a foreign country
Walking into a men's john by mistake
Being 28 years old and wearing braces
Having small breasts
Being married and retaining close male friends
Not going crazy in a painfully menial job
Living away from boyfriend/husband

It's good to know those occasions when we *do* feel competent, especially when others may not. So use this opportunity to find out about yourself:

Time for Yourself #9

Each evening for one week jot down the times during that day when you *did* manage potentially stressful situations.

Date   *SUDS Level*   *Situation*

Dealing with Your Tensions

Do you remember a time in your life when a serious, tension-producing situation was suddenly terminated by a joke that brought forth peals of laughter? Or has your mind ever "stopped" when the pressure was so intense that you simply couldn't think?

Humor and thinking are incompatible with tension, but they *are* compatible with relaxation. It is just about impossible to laugh and remain tense. Laughter is even exaggerated at times when it occurs as a source of relief. And while our minds may block at words, names, or thoughts when we are "under fire," relaxation—the antithesis of tension—helps retrieve our memory.

These facts give us a clue not only to the value of humor but to the importance of relaxation as a way to handle stress. The beauty of it is that we can work on relaxation techniques by ourselves.

SPECIFIC RELAXATION TECHNIQUES

Mid-morning and afternoon breaks for employed adults and recess periods for children are a part of our world. But even though they signal changes of activity, they do not always mean a time of relaxation. People may still be surrounded by noise, encounters with others, personal demands on their free time, or other distractions and pressures. As a result, some industries concerned with overall productivity arrange calming "relief" rooms in which employees can simply relax quietly and then return to their jobs with more energy for work. Certain schools concerned with children's need for reducing tensions help them adjust with a "time out" place in which to relax alone.

People seek ways to relieve tension and relax without realizing it. You may recall that Samantha's *SUDS* level record showed she interspersed window-shopping and stopping at the water cooler between periods of pressure. People may also function at a high level of tension so often that they come to accept and even depend on it as part of their life style; for instance, Dorie, mentioned earlier, who estimated her average *SUDS* level as 77.

Integrating relaxation into our lives helps us "refuel" or regain control. You are familiar with the relaxation benefits of exercising (jogging, swimming, walking) or meditation (transcendental meditation, yoga). You can also take time each day, even for a few moments, just to feel lazy. Try it now. Sit passively. Relax your shoulders. Release the joints in your arms, your hips, your knees. Close your eyes. Ignore any distracting thoughts that creep in and allow them to slip by. . . .

Progressive relaxation. Combining elements of exercise and meditation, progressive relaxation is a method for tensing and relaxing groups of body muscles while you concentrate on how it feels. Sit or lie down in a comfortable place by yourself and close your eyes. Then concentrate on tightening, holding for several seconds, and letting go of one muscle group at a time while deliberately thinking about how it feels. Gradually work your way through your body. If you like, try relaxing in this manner for ten to twenty minutes each day. The following instructions will help you.

RELAXATION INSTRUCTIONS	
Muscle Groups	*Tension Exercises*
1. the dominant hand 2. the other hand	make a tight fist
3. the dominant arm 4. the other arm	curl your arm up; tighten the bicep
5. upper face and scalp	raise eyebrows as high as possible
6. center face	squint eyes and wrinkle nose
7. lower face	smile in a false, exaggerated way; clench teeth
8. neck	pull head slightly forward, then relax; pull head slightly back, then relax
9. chest and shoulders	pull shoulders back till the blades almost touch, then relax; pull shoulders forward all the way, then relax
10. abdomen	make abdomen tight and hard
11. buttocks	tighten together
12. upper right leg 13. upper left leg	stretch leg out from you, tensing both upper and lower muscles
14. lower right leg 15. lower left leg	pull toes up toward you
16. right foot 17. left foot	curl toes down and away from you

(continued on next page)

First for each muscle group

Tense the muscles and hold for 5 seconds.

Feel the tension. Notice it carefully.

Now release. Let the tension slide away, all away.

Feel the difference

Notice the pleasant warmth of relaxation.

Now repeat the sequences with the same group.

Repeat again. Do the sequence three times for each group of muscles.

Tense. Release. Learn the difference. Feel the warmth of relaxation.

Then for the whole body

Now tense all the muscles together and hold for 5 seconds.

Feel the tension, notice it carefully, then release. Let all tension slide away.

Notice any remaining tension.

Release it.

Take a deep breath. Say softly to yourself "relax," as you breathe out slowly.

Remain totally relaxed.

Repeat breathing in and then out slowly, saying "relax," staying perfectly relaxed.

Do this three times.

The exercise has ended. Enjoy the relaxation.

In your daily life, in many situations

Notice your body's tension. Identify the tense muscle groups. Say softly to yourself "relax." Relax the tense group. Feel the relaxation and enjoy it.

From *Self-Directed Behavior,* 3rd ed. by D. L. Watson and R. G. Tharp. Copyright © 1981 by Wadsworth, Inc. Reprinted by permission of Brooks/Cole Publishing Company, Monterey, California. (Adapted from *Insight vs. Desensitization in Psychotherapy* by G. L. Paul. Copyright © 1977 by Stanford University Press. Reprinted by permission.)

Instant relaxation. But, you say, many times when I need to relax there's no place to exercise, no privacy for meditation or progressive relaxation. I may be driving my car or sitting in a room full of people. While it doesn't offer the range of muscle involvement that progressive relaxation does, deep breathing is an alternative. It is simple to perform inconspic-uously almost anytime.

Try it. Take a deep breath. (It is best with your mouth closed.) Hold it. Count to three slowly. Then *gradually* release it completely. Another time. Hold your breath. Count to three slowly. Now gradually let it out. Sometimes people concentrate on words such as re-lax, ea-sy, let-go, or others of their choice to enhance concentration on their tension reduction as they breathe in and out.

A simple extension of this procedure increases its effec-tiveness. Once again take a deep breath. Pause and hold. Now without releasing any air take a second deep breath. Hold for a slow count of three and gradually release. By taking in additional oxygen more body cavity muscles are used. Doing this several times is an instant relaxer for that part of your body. After you have completed your deep breathing you may extend your relaxation by yawning and stretching.

People can use breathing exercises in a variety of situ-ations—while waiting for a stop light to change when driving, during an important interview, before appearing in front of an audience, prior to confronting someone about a problem. For periods of minor and normal tension during the course of daily activities, deep breathing can be combined with pro-gressive relaxation. It helps to keep your *SUDS* level in check.

BUILDING A HIERARCHY

Now we turn to overcoming obstacles in our daily lives that make us scared or tense, and look at ways to intervene to help control our feelings.

The Fear/Stress Principle: To help overcome fear or tension about a situation, very gradually increase your ex-posure to the situation while you are otherwise relaxed, secure, and rewarded. Since it is impossible to be anxious and relaxed at the same time, you want to combine comfort with your fear. This helps keep your *SUDS* level lowered. As you find you are able to control it, you can then very gradually increase exposure to your fear without freaking out.

Donna is married and the mother of a 9-month-old infant

and a 3½-year-old daughter. Her life is largely domestic. "I was an office manager for five years and I know there's a fast-paced life out there. But for the past four years I've devoted my life solely to my family. Now I don't feel I have anything important to say to people anymore. I especially feel uncomfortable with men I meet at social gatherings with my husband."

Donna's starter goal is to overcome her fear of talking about herself to men in social situations. What type of intervention plan might help her change? What target behavior might initiate the process of helping her face up to this fear while at the same time keeping her relatively relaxed?

Donna reasons that her own parties give her a sense of control that she does not feel when talking with men elsewhere. (Some women feel just the opposite.) She scrutinizes the guest list for a dinner party she and her husband have planned and describes her feelings. "I picked out one man who has always been nice to me. Then I agonized over what I would talk about. My inclination is to turn the conversation immediately back to the other person. Then I decided—my self-change group. It's my only project outside my home."

Donna has a target behavior—to talk with Allen at the party and tell him about her weekly meetings. Yes, her *SUDS* level would elevate some, but no, not too much with Allen. She thinks she can handle it. She decides it would be a good idea to mention problems she has learned about that make communication difficult between women and men.

Donna's talk with Allen proved to be more rewarding than she expected. "It was great. I even explained the fear I was working on—that is, talking about myself. He told me he prefers talking with women than with most men because he feels men tend to depersonalize and talk about abstract ideas. Then a light went on: It's not just my inadequacy. Even Allen doesn't always feel secure. That made me more relaxed."

While the results of Donna's first target behavior are a resounding success, she must now continue her intervention plan. She needs to expand from this initial success by gradually increasing her exposure to other similar situations while keeping her *SUDS* level intact. This requires a series of small target behaviors of gradually increasing difficulty. Accomplishing one at a time, she then can move slowly up a ladder to her goal. If her *SUDS* level increases, she may repeat some target steps more than once or create substeps. This is what building a hierarchy is all about.

Pleased with herself, Donna wastes no time arranging other steps when the same friends plan another party. The next level in her hierarchy is to listen to what a small group of men talk about and contribute to the conversation. So joining three men talking about taxes, she bravely interjects an idea she read about in a weekly news magazine. They discuss it briefly, but her *SUDS* level elevates so much that she does not talk clearly and realizes that step was too big.

Another target behavior is to initiate a conversation with men on both sides of her at dinner. When one man she knows only slightly asks her about herself, she tells him about her workshop instead of turning the conversation immediately back to him. Since this one-to-one conversation is easier than talking about taxes to several men, she realizes that reversing the order of her hierarchy, and possibly building in intermediate steps, would have been wise.

As her *SUDS* level stays down, Donna can expand her conversation topics and talk to more people. Other women, especially those feeling confined during the child-rearing years, have mentioned related starter goals dealing with conversational skills. These include keeping topics on issues (as opposed to children, household cleaning aids, personal complaints) and maintaining a regular reading schedule about current events for sources of conversation topics.

A feeling of accomplishment is vital to Donna's success. She recognizes that she is improving, and her self-change group cheers her on.

Success often comes not only from trying to compete with yourself or with others to see how brave you can be or how much you can accomplish under pressure, but from the realization that *without* intense pressure you may do even better because you feel more comfortable.

Eva's starter goal is to overcome fear of authority figures, particularly her political science professor. This is important to her because she wants to enter a special program for which an interview with the professor is required. "My fear is based upon years of admiration for a person with high prestige," says Eva. "That woman symbolizes my dreams and ambitions. I want to lower my anxiety around her so I come across well when I talk to her in her office. That's my goal."

At the start, Eva's only contact with the professor is as a student in a large lecture class. Below is the hierarchy Eva developed and the comments she wrote as she progressed up her ladder:

1. **Move my seat from the rear to the front of the room.** (Seats are not assigned. I moved halfway up one day, to the front the next. The second time raised my *SUDS* level considerably so I did nothing further the next three periods until I was completely comfortable sitting in front of the podium.)

2. **Linger after class and listen to others ask questions.** (This took another three periods before I was completely at ease. At first I moved in too fast and my *SUDS* level zoomed up—so I immediately backed away and stayed only a few minutes the first day. The next time I hung back, felt better, and inched forward as students asked her questions, telling myself it was okay and to stay calm. By the third day I was still a silent participant but really became absorbed in what was being said.)

3. **Attend a special-topic seminar with the professor as guest speaker.** (This was not planned originally in my hierarchy but it turned out to fit in beautifully. The group was small and informal. While I did not speak up, I sat near her and my *SUDS* level remained low after some initial fluctuation.)

4. **Plan a question I can ask her after class.** (I figured out a logical, simple question about an assignment and rehearsed it several times to myself. Then I plunged in. When she answered she smiled at me a little. Encouraging!)

5. **Find her office and walk by it often enough to be comfortable.** (I did this three separate times over several days. I looked around until the surroundings were familiar to me.)

6. **Phone her secretary for an appointment.** (Scary, because the dye was cast! I reminded myself to keep thinking positively—"Baby, you've come a long way.")

7. **Organize the interview.** (I knew this was important, so after I had my main points worked out I really took two additional steps. Alone in my own room I closed my eyes and imagined the whole interview—what she might say, how I might respond. I tried different approaches, and I tried to imagine the worst and the best. I wanted to anticipate everything I could. Then I role-played the interview with Patty. She is a good friend who

takes the course, too. We tried multi-possibilities, so many that I couldn't believe we had missed anything, or if we had that it would make a difference.)

8. **Confront the interview itself.** (My immediate goal was to keep my *SUDS* level down. Not to start blocking. I went early so as not to be rushed and brought along the campus newspaper to read. I remembered my deep breathing in the outer office but forgot about it later. I also allowed another student to go ahead of me so I wouldn't be intimidated by someone waiting. I reassured myself. Things like "Eva, you are as well prepared as you'll ever be. Relax, kid.")

"As I look back now I wonder why I ever was so scared of that woman. The interview was a let-down after all my preparation, but I sure was glad I'd done it. It didn't go entirely as I expected, but the only time I felt like a klutz was when I tripped over the carpet in the outer office, but by then it was all over."

Her feeling of anticlimax to the interview is a real tribute to Eva's solid preparation. She can now extend her starter goals to other authority figures if she wants to persist in overcoming this fear. Continuing to build success into her efforts is important at each point along the way, not only by taking very small steps but also by remaining reasonably comfortable and having support from others as she improves.

Eva's hierarchy really contains far more than the eight steps she lists, for her intervals also include substeps—each one really a small target behavior of its own. Sometimes hierarchies are simpler. It depends on how many steps are needed in a ladder toward a specific goal in order to keep your *SUDS* level from elevating.

Eva employs four devices that are useful to insert in a hierarchy. We will look at each and see how other women use them.

Self-rehearsing steps. Practicing by yourself before you take action helps keep your *SUDS* level down. For example, Vanessa, just separated from her husband, feels strongly about what she will and won't discuss with other people about her marriage. By rehearsing to herself the explanation she is comfortable with, she becomes less anxious mentioning her change in status to others.

Role-playing steps. Simulating the situation by acting it out with others, especially with repetitions and variations, helps a person stay relaxed in the actual performance. It is a form of rehearsal. Leslie, whose *SUDS* level elevates when she is introduced to people, role-plays listening for conversational cues with her housemates. Six-foot-tall Peggy role-plays with her brother the ways she can respond to remarks about her height. Bess role-plays with her best friend talking to her teenage daughter about coming home late.

Imagining steps. Sometimes it is simply impossible to practice relaxing in the actual feared situation; for example, when suddenly running into a former boyfriend or experiencing the discomfort of long silences in real conversations. So in lieu of "live" steps, you can deliberately *imagine* your feared situation while simultaneously using relaxation techniques to keep your *SUDS* level down. Aggie, working up the ladder of a hierarchy to overcome her fear of taking taxis, spends ten minutes each day for several days visually imagining the details of her first ride alone until she feels relatively relaxed thinking about it. Pairing imagery with relaxation makes the real event, when it occurs, less awesome. People adept at imagery can imagine touch, smell, sound, voices, even colors. Try it in a quiet place with your eyes closed.

Imagery is also used to emphasize the rewards of facing a stressful situation. Suann, working up her courage to ask a certain man for a date, spends several quiet periods imagining vividly how much she will enjoy telling certain women friends what she has done. And Marta, frightened of others' reactions if she admits she has a serious drinking problem, imagines how relieved she will feel when she no longer needs to cover up.

In self-change, you will find that imagery has many uses. If your imagination works overtime, make sure it's working for you, not against you.

Self-coaching steps. When we help others through stressful periods, the most obvious and often the best form of encouragement comes from our words of support. Yet we are only now learning that we can help ourselves as well as others through what we say. As she initiates her contacts with her political science professor, Eva judiciously uses coaching—

self-talk—to help herself stay relaxed, to cue herself to stay optimistic, and to give herself general reassurance. Here are some self-statements other women have made to cope specifically with tension:

> "Stay calm. Take deep breaths. Keep that *SUDS* level down."
> "Hang in there. It's going to be okay."
> "It will be over soon. Just a little longer."
> "Concentrate on what you are doing rather than on how you are feeling."
> "One step at a time. That's all you need."
> "Five years (or five minutes) from now it won't matter."
> "Stop and think. It could be worse."
> "Nice going. You're handling it."
> "Steady there. Hold on. You can cope."
> "You're doing better. That's what's important."

Another world opens up to us when we deliberately give ourselves the same kind of verbal backing we give others. Used correctly it is a valuable skill. You will learn about other uses in Chapter thirteen.

Rehearsal, role playing, imagery, and self-talk incorporated into a hierarchy all contribute to our ability to relax and cope.

Choosing a Fear to Overcome

You are now ready to embark on your own hierarchy project. In selecting a fear to work on, keep the following thoughts in mind.

NO PHOBIAS, PLEASE

Select a fear from everyday stressful situations you encounter rather than from large freak-out problems that may require professional help. Our main purpose is to overcome fears or stresses our socialization as females allows or encourages us to retain.

HOW EAGER ARE YOU?

Increase your chances of success by being highly motivated. Strip away advice from others and ask yourself "What fear do *I* want to overcome?"

SOME FEARS WORTH KEEPING

Some fears are important to hang onto. For example, the fear that you don't spend enough time with your children may give you incentive to arrange higher quality time with them. The fear of hitchhiking or rape may help you remain more aware of your surroundings. Such fears, if not exaggerated, are assets.

ASK YOURSELF: IS THIS
THE REAL FEAR?

Sometimes it's hard to figure out what the real fear is. Is it a fear of sex or a fear of getting pregnant? A fear of being a mother or a fear of losing your independence? A fear of authority figures or a fear of men?

Faith, married to a man with whom she runs a printing business, spends a week logging conditions under which she thinks she is afraid to make decisions. She wants to find target behaviors to work on. Instead she is surprised to find that she really has no trouble making decisions. Her decisions pertain especially to her part of the business, and people respect her judgment—everyone, that is, except her husband. He routinely reacts by dissenting and at times becoming frighteningly angry. When she understands it is really his anger that makes her afraid to state decisions she has made, Faith quickly changes starter goals to work on ways to strengthen communication with her husband and give stronger support to decisions he makes in his part of the business, hoping that he will then be less defensive about hers. These are quite different projects.

AN ALTERNATIVE WAY

Faith's switch from working on a hierarchy about a fear (of making decisions) to working on ways to alleviate the reason for it (her husband's insecurity) illustrates another way to cope with anxiousness; that is, to build other attitudes and actions that do away with the basis for the fear. Thus fears such as being considered ugly or old, of applying for a job, or of being "just a housewife (or a face, a body, an ornament)," might then be dealt with by thinking of them as fears that will lessen or disappear provided certain positive behaviors are developed.

Time for Yourself #10

Construct and work on a hierarchy for overcoming a fear of your own using as many skills as possible from what you have just read.

Hierarchy Target Steps   *Comments on Progress*

Helping Others Handle Fear

Understanding the hierarchy steps enables us to help others face their fears in the same way. Not only can we help children cope differently, but occasionally adults as well.

Sara and Richard Benson have a nineteen-year traditional marriage they have evaluated as "strong." But as their children grow older and Sara reads more about women's concerns, she feels compelled to make some changes in her life for her personal growth. Richard counters her initial attempts at increased independence first with dismay, then with hostility. Sara's reaction is that he is rigid and chauvinistic, and it prompts her to talk with a marriage counselor.

Sara views Richard with more compassion when she understands that her changing threatens him. So as she continues to plan for herself, she also tries to act in ways that will help him cope with his fears.

Sara knows that tears or anger from her will only raise the tension level, thereby eliciting negative and difficult-to-revoke responses from Richard. So for now she tries to release her own feelings of stress elsewhere. She also thinks through a series of steps that will slowly increase her autonomy, beginning with a real estate course she plans to take at a community college. She tells Richard about it when they are on a long walk together and both of them are relaxed. (She wants the conditions to be as comfortable as possible.) "It's going to be great having something to talk to you about besides the house and kids," she says calmly but firmly. "We'll both benefit."

Sara does not seek Richard's opinion about taking the course because she knows it will be negative. But she makes it clear she wants to include him in her plans. She is determined to make him as comfortable and nonthreatened as possible as she takes gradual steps toward growth for herself. Whether she succeeds in convincing him that their marriage will benefit depends on many things, but the chances are greater if the panic buttons for both of them are controlled. Sara therefore works on two hierarchies—one for herself and one for the husband she loves.

Fear controls us unless we control it. The sooner we notice symptoms of fear or stress, the more likely we can deal with the anxiety—both in ourselves and in others.

Part 3

BUILDING YOUR OWN KIND OF LIFE

Are you ready to change your own world? Your personal life is what you choose to make it. Now you will look at ways either to strengthen actions you already like or to build entirely new ones. Chapters six, seven, and eight discuss three basic strategies: arranging reinforcement, modeling others, and recognizing cues in your surroundings. While you view each one separately, eventually you will combine them in your own way. The results will help you advance toward your goals.

CHAPTER SIX

Successful
Self-Mothering

> I must get something out of the way I am or I
> wouldn't be this way.
>
> Jill

> Me tells *me* I'm doing better? Do you really think
> I'd believe it?
>
> Claire

Sometimes our culture works in women's favor. Many say our greatest strength is nurturance—caring about others and being empathetic. So now we are going to apply this strength to ourselves.

Self-nurturance is often misunderstood. It *does not* mean justifying personal indulgences that disregard the feelings of others. It *does* mean nourishing our own needs as well as preserving our own pleasures. As with assertiveness, it does not mean ignoring the rights of others, but it does mean making certain our own rights are not abused. Each balances the other. Too often in the past we have ignored ourselves, and that is why some have called this need for balance *responsible selfishness.*

We are going to pay more attention to our own accomplishments, acknowledging them rather than being self-effacing. We are not going to put ourselves down when we fail, because we know that failure, too, can be a contributor to growth and that self-chastisement is nonproductive. Finally, we are going to use self-nurturance very systematically to make positive changes in our own lives. To do this, we need to know about reinforcement.

Changing with Systematic Self-Support

The Reinforcement Principle: To initiate or strengthen an action, reinforce it (or any tendencies toward it) as soon as possible following each improved performance until that action is learned. Let's look at the key ideas in this principle.

REINFORCEMENT AS PAYOFF

Rewards, praise, pleasurable experiences—any positive consequences you receive whenever you take action in the direction of your goals—constitute positive reinforcement. Maxine says, "Hey, Nan, how about congratulating me when I swim by myself?" thereby arranging approval from her friend for increasing her own independence. Evelyn offers herself a pleasurable payoff for washing the car by driving it to a place to dry off where she can sunbathe at the same time. Michele says reinforcingly to herself, "You're keeping your priorities straight," when she doesn't lower her standards for a babysitter despite time pressure from her fast-track consulting position.

Used properly, reinforcement becomes a major tool for self-development and moves us forward.

DOING BETTER IS WHAT COUNTS

Since women are often perfectionists, one of our difficulties is recognizing our gradual improvements, for perfectionists tend to monitor their *im*perfections, noting mistakes and areas where problems still exist rather than keeping track of ways they are doing better.

Don't wait until you have changed completely to reward yourself. Any actions in the direction of the new behavior are important to recognize, for this boosts the desire to continue. Isabelle points out to herself that she is less depressed now than she was two months ago, even though she still has periods of crying when thinking about the tragic loss of her baby. Marcy, observing that she doesn't forget what she has to say as often when talking to her boss, shares her increased sense of confidence with her office mate: "You know, Dave, I only blocked once when I talked to her. That's progress."

PEANUTS® by Charles M. Schulz

EMPHASIZE GRADUAL IMPROVEMENT RATHER THAN PROBLEMS

Sherry notes to herself that her tennis serve is stronger despite the fact that she still doesn't hit the ball with the power she desires.

Noting even small improvements and rewarding them strengthens our chances for change.

TIMING

When you receive reinforcement is as important as the reinforcement itself. Arrange for it as soon as possible following any positive change. *Establish a linkage between the improved actions and a pleasurable result.* Then that new response is more likely to take place again in the future. Determined to learn routine house carpentry, Brenda *promptly* praises herself for following the directions to put up a bathroom towel rack. "Wonderful, B. You figured it out without yelling for help!" Pat, instead of clamming up when she has a disagreement with her boyfriend, tries to explain her feelings to him and is *immediately gratified* when he tells her he now understands better why she feels the way she does. Pris promises herself a fifteen-minute break *as soon as* she completes the next section of her committee report. Reinforcement usually strengthens whatever behavior immediately precedes it.

Self-mothering is really nurturance coupled with a sense of personal responsibility. Whether you build in your own gratifications or arrange them from others, you are self-managing when you make certain you receive payoff at the right time.

Making It Work

You know how to find target behaviors from starter goals. Now see how to select rewards and tie them to your performance.

SELECTING YOUR REWARDS

"I did it! Chalk one up for me!" "I, Sunny, handled that situation without any excuses. I deserve congratulations." "Bet-

90

ter, better, better. I *am* doing better." "It's really good that I'm not leaning on Jack so much."

In self-change the most frequent kind of reinforcement you give yourself comes from positive self-statements of honest praise. Their ready availability for creating a positive association with your new actions makes them especially desirable.

So brag a little to yourself. Don't be bashful. It may take a little doing not to feel silly, but when you do it you will see it can make a real difference in the way you feel.

Speak to yourself without put-downs. Say, "You did a fine job on that," but don't add, "Bet you can't do it again." Tell yourself, "You're not stupid," but don't add "this time." Be kind.

If praise alone is insufficient, then turn to other gratifications. Look over your pleasures lists from Chapter four. Those items often trigger practical ideas for rewards or are useful themselves. Give separate rewards for each target, except for praise. Sincere, honest praise, either from yourself or from others, is almost always helpful. When you consider nonverbal rewards, answer these questions:

Does it reward you (not just others around you)? Oftentimes women talk themselves into thinking that a reward someone close to them would like rewards them as well.

Kay at 34 is a widow with two young children. She works three mornings a week for a mail-order firm while a baby-sitter stays with her youngest child. On Saturday afternoons Kay's sister stays with the children while Kay visits friends or tends to errands. Ordinarily this routine is satisfactory, she says, unless an unusual situation arises.

Recently Kay decided to paint her living room. "I've put the job off so often. Just simple procrastination. To do that job with the children around seems overwhelming. But" — firmly— "I'm determined to do it during this next week, and if I finish before the weekend, my gift to myself is to take the children to the beach Saturday afternoon."

Note what Kay is doing. She takes away from herself her only free time and replaces it with child care, already a burden in her circumscribed life style. Her personal time, especially when she has so little social life, is vital to maintain her emotional balance during a difficult period. Treating her children by giving them an opportunity to vary their usual activities is important, but her own special time should not be sacrificed. Kay might better save her Saturday afternoon for herself and take her children to the beach another day.

Women who are the primary caretakers of young children can learn too well to identify with others' needs and neglect their own. If they do not look out for themselves, too, suddenly one day they will ask themselves "Who am I?" and not have any answers.

Is your reward readily accessible? Charlotte, 57, anticipates a Christmas visit from her mother, who is 81. Their relationship has never flourished, but now Charlotte actually dreads their time together since it always degenerates into "one round of grim encounters after another."

"She's argumentative, and I rise to the bait," says Charlotte. "I know this, but it's so hard not to take a stand. Mother obviously isn't going to change, so it's really a matter of how *I* react. Ignoring her comments is the only way, but believe me, it isn't easy."

Thus, Charlotte's goal: to remain calm and unresponsive during her mother's visit on those occasions when she thinks an argument might be prevented as a result. Deep breathing exercises, she decides, will help keep her SUDS level lowered. "If I succeed in making her visit reasonably pleasant," Charlotte adds, "I've promised myself season tickets to the summer theater series, and I'll deserve it!"

But the tickets cannot be used until the season starts in June, six months away. What Charlotte really needs is an immediately accessible reward to create the necessary linkage we talked about earlier. To her close friend she might say, "Look, Dede, I need your help when mother is here. When I phone you and report the number of times I've prevented arguments, just tell me I'm improving or even succeeding. It will help me a lot, knowing I have your encouragement. Then let's plan a movie together later." This way Charlotte has both immediate reward and something to look forward to in the near future as well.

Is your reward strong enough? Changing yourself can be compared to Watty Piper's children's story, *The Little Engine*

That Could. Remember at the beginning the engine is at the bottom of the mountain and starts with great difficulty ("I . . . . . think . . . . I . . . . . can. . . . . . I . . . . . think . . . . . I . . . . . can. . . ."). Progress is slow at first but as the engine nears the top of the mountain, its speed increases slightly and the task is less arduous ("I think . . . I . . . can. . . . I . . . think . . . I . . . can. . . .") until finally the engine is over the top and speeds downhill with a sense of accomplishment ("I thought I could. I thought I could.").

If the degrees of difficulty throughout your change tasks were charted, they would most likely look like the shape of a bell-shaped mountain with the most difficult part—the time you exert the most effort—at the beginning of a steep incline. The closer you come to the top the easier it is to follow through. Later, improvement takes over and spurs you on rapidly, almost as if you were speeding downhill.

It makes sense, then, that the rewards you need at first are stronger than those you need later. Extrinsic rewards—anything from a visit with friends to food or even money—may be needed to initiate new actions. (People have even been known to give a friend money that is paid back to them as improvement occurs.) When your goal-directed actions increase, other less powerful reinforcers can and should be substituted and then gradually eliminated as the new behavior takes over. Occasional reinforcement with a new action that has been well enough learned is more powerful than constant reinforcement. Eventually your own success carries you along with no planned rewards necessary.

Might your reward hurt others? It happens. Kate rewards herself by listening to her hi fi but inconveniences others who want to sleep. Carin rewards herself with a day in the city even though her child is sick at home. Arlene rewards herself by buying a flower bowl with money from the family entertainment fund. When you choose rewards for yourself, consider their broader implications.

What if no reward seems right? Don't give up yet. If a reward doesn't fit, you might try *imagining* one that does. Daphne, an editor with heavy responsibilities, is overcommitted on a project for which she is responsible and is concerned about keeping up with demands from her regular work. She selects as a starter goal facing one day at a time to prevent feeling overwhelmed. To reinforce her efforts toward this goal, whenever she stays calm under fire Daphne deliberately takes a minute to imagine herself being sought out by her peers because of her ability to be philosophical about life's pressures. She feels her imagined reinforcement is more powerful than other rewards because it emphasizes results bearing on her starter goal.

If you prefer to be less fanciful, turn to activities you engage in routinely to see if they might help you perform your target behavior. They should occur frequently. While they do not need to be reinforcing (although that would help), they should not be punishing either. Often they are simply "neutral" activities in your life. Driving to work, picking up your child from school, grocery shopping, doing laundry, watching TV, washing your hair, putting on makeup, even preparing a meal are all possibilities. The idea is to use the routine activity in lieu of a reward, timing it to occur immediately following your target behavior. These are examples other women have used:

> balancing a checkbook before attending a meeting
> sewing on a button before putting on a blouse
> doing exercises before making the bed
> writing a letter before reading the mail
> repairing the faucet before taking off for work
> reading the financial section of the newspaper before the front page
> making a decision before leaving the apartment

Are tokens effective as rewards? Tokens represent rewards, nudging you on after each improved performance. They take many forms—check marks, tallies, coins, poker chips. The real reward is simply delayed until a certain number of tokens accumulate.

Kari uses paper clips as tokens. They are convenient because she ordinarily keeps a leather purse nearby that has two easily accessible side pockets. Kari grudgingly admits that she has difficulty relating to women. She prefers men's company in just about any situation. She feels uncomfortable lunching "just with women" and always turns down invitations to play tennis with women after work. As she becomes more sensitive both to women's problems and to her own reliance on men, she decides she wants to change. Telling herself to do so simply doesn't work, so she goes about it more deliberately. Her target behavior: to increase the number of questions she asks the women in her office about their own concerns (as opposed to keeping the conversation on trivia or dominating it herself).

Kari's method: Each time she asks a substantive question of a woman co-worker she transfers a paper clip from one side pocket in her purse to the other, thereby keeping track of her question-asking. Contrived? Yes. Far-fetched? For some people, certainly. But for Kari the paper clips serve as a reminder of her goal. "Hot little things, burning a hole in my purse." Kari plans to reward herself with a long-distance phone call to a friend (male, of course) after ten paper clips have changed pockets.

The reinforcement Kari finds from talking seriously with two of the women is so eye-opening that after moving the first seven clips she stops. They have primed her desire to continue on her own as her indifference gives way to a recognition of common interests. Kari no longer needs tokens toward an extrinsic reward. (With others, tokens might prove insufficient.)

Typically, after a predetermined number of tokens are earned, people do follow through with a "real" reward for themselves. One advantage to this system is that fewer actual rewards are necessary since tokens are used first. However, the main advantage is that tokens can be made easily accessible, whereas the rewards we prefer may not. This way we can anticipate later rewards for which tokens serve as a down payment.

APPLYING REWARDS WITH KNOW-HOW

After selecting your rewards you are ready to use the Reinforcement Principle. Here are the ground rules:

- Reinforce any new action immediately or as soon as possible until it is learned. When you catch yourself doing better, make certain you arrange positive consequences.

- After an action is learned, gradually eliminate reinforcement. Improvement becomes its own reward.
- If you slip back into the old habit, the new learning is not complete and more sustained reinforcement is needed. Occasional rewards are powerful only provided a new action is well enough developed.

INCREASING THE ODDS: ADDITIONAL SUPPORTS

The following aids can also contribute to your success:

Ask others to help. As Penny's awareness grows, she looks more closely at her relationship with Peter, her boyfriend, and decides she relies on him in many ways that do not benefit their relationship. "Pete often drives me to my job. I find myself asking his opinion on everything before I make up my mind. I usually tag along when he plays basketball with the guys on Saturday, sitting on the sideline to watch. Things like that."

Penny chooses a target behavior to work on and decides, characteristically, that she needs Peter's help to make the changes she wants. "I talked it over with him. He knows this is good for both of us, and he has agreed to help me.

"Here's what I'm asking of Pete: 'Support me when I'm trying to be more self-sufficient. Somehow recognize any little successes I have, maybe with a glance or a word of understanding or sincere praise. Be encouraging. Whatever the recognition, give it as soon as possible. And those times when I'm trying but don't succeed, please don't tease me or say anything sarcastic. I'll know without your putting it on the seven o'clock news.' "

Initially Penny needs to rely on her boyfriend. What she is doing is to *alter* the way she depends on him. As she becomes more self-assured she will want to rely on him less.

Many people find it important to rely on others for support, especially at first when changing is most difficult. With women this is logical when we think how females are socialized to remain dependent, especially on males. In an attempt to buck their socialization and lean less on men, some women try to shift their dependence to other women as a step toward autonomy. But the final step comes when we rely on our own decisions, asking help of others in limited situations but relying mainly on our own judgment. Penny's altered dependence on Peter is a step in the right direction.

Monitor your improvement. Logging, counting responses, rating feelings, charting, writing structured diaries—all are potential sources of good feelings to spur you on. When you record, your improvement becomes both more obvious and more objective, and if you don't improve you can better analyze what went wrong.

Remember hierarchies and rehearsals. A little risk-taking accompanies most change. There is that built-in comfort of staying as we are that prompts Jill to say, "I must *get* something out of the way I am or I wouldn't be this way." Since risk-taking contains elements of fear or stress, you may want to introduce a hierarchy using rehearsal steps and *SUDS* levels. Role-playing or visual imagery, for example, can help you become accustomed to the change before you actually face it.

Margo began her career as a bank teller at 22 and advanced rapidly because of her ability to grasp ideas and work with numbers. After five years she is supervising fourteen employees. Yearly performance evaluations by her superiors confirm that Margo does well in all respects but one. She has difficulty delegating responsibility and often ends up doing jobs herself that should be given to others.

Many women have trouble using power in constructive ways with others. We may be ambivalent or simply not like to use it at all, perhaps associating it with exploitation or even with violence. For whatever reasons, many of us perceive power as masculine and feel uncomfortable with it. Yet in the still-male world of Margo's potentially bright future, she needs to reconcile her negative feelings about power with her own job performance. This involves learning to delegate responsibility.

Margo proceeds with her first target behavior. She enlists in a workshop in which specific management skills are dramatized by the group, including how to delegate to others in various situations. Next she begins to adapt the methods she prefers to her own job situation, rehearsing the dividing of responsibilities and direction-giving each time in advance. She rewards herself with positive self-statements for trying, especially since she is met by resistance from her subordinates when she stops doing their work. As they gradually assume more duties and her own sense of sureness grows, rewards become automatic. Her concluding remarks: "I never want to 'control' people. But part of *my* responsibility is to see that others do theirs. Really just another skill to learn."

Consider modeling and cueing. In the following two chapters you will read about two other facilitators for building changes in your life, modeling and cueing. They combine well with reinforcement and help increase your reinforcement repertory.

Time for Yourself #11

Select one starter goal to strengthen or develop and subdivide it into target behaviors. (You may choose goals from Projects #2 and #3 in Chapter two.) Before you begin your change project, decide on appropriate reward(s) that you can give yourself immediately following each improved performance. Start on one target at a time, gradually completing several as you work toward your starter goal.

IF IT DOESN'T WORK, WHAT THEN?

Stop. Before you do anything else, remember: no self-defeating comments. Perhaps we can find the reason.

Check your target and rewards. Glance back to Chapter two and answer the questions about choosing the best target. Next, answer the questions about selecting your rewards, discussed early in this chapter. Finally, answer these questions:

Are you being reinforced in more than one direction? Here is the stuff that double binds are made of—in this instance, opposing sources of reinforcement. (Double binds also result from opposing sources of unpleasantness.) Ask yourself what your rewards are for *not* changing to a new behavior and you may understand why you are having trouble with it.

Inga, a divorced mother who returned to college now that her children, ages 6 and 10, are both in school, has as her goal spending time with them each afternoon when they all arrive home. She says, "It's precious time for me. I love hearing about their days."

However, Inga has difficulty following through with her plan and finally realizes why. "I badly need a little time to adjust from a tough day in my own classes to being a mom again. Getting home, going to my room alone, and relaxing for fifteen minutes first is a great temptation and powerfully rewarding."

When Inga realizes why the new schedule creates a conflict, she delays her time with the children "unless they have pressing problems" and does take a few minutes to relax alone. "This gives me a chance to get my head together first."

For any action you wish to change, examine what payoffs result from your present behavior. Think, for instance, what reinforcement a woman needs to counter if she wants to stop exaggerating when she talks to others, or if she decides it is wise not to give so much advice to her children. *Her present behavior holds some rewards or she wouldn't continue it.* When she knows the reasons for it, she may be able to arrange for the conflicting reinforcement to end, to be minimized, or (as with Inga) to structure the situation differently.

Do you withhold your reward until your actions improve? Delaying gratification is never easy, but when you are the only one controlling your reinforcement, you alone deal with your conscience. Do these phrases sound familiar? "One time won't matter," "I'll begin tomorrow instead of today," "There's got to be a better way," "Nobody knows what I'm trying to do anyhow," "I'm not even sure I want to change." After any of these thoughts it's all too tempting to grab the reward without waiting for the improvement.

Recall that a reward tends to increase the behavior immediately preceding it and you see what happens: You reward yourself for giving in. It follows that giving in the next time is easier because you have started to reward giving-in behavior. For example, Marcia decides to reward herself by spending an afternoon in her favorite museum provided she attends all sessions of a two-day conference. However, her persistence is poor and she defaults, going to the museum instead of one of the meetings. In the future she is apt to find it even easier to skip a conference session because she has reinforced herself for nonattendance.

We all have this problem occasionally. What can we do

about it? How can we control delaying gratification until we really deserve it? The following strategies might help you.

First, tell others what reward you plan for what actions. With someone else involved, you are less likely to cheat. Marcia can say to her friend, "Jessie, I've decided to go to the museum if I attend all the sessions." She might even add courageously, "I'm telling you so I won't cheat on myself." Written contracts with others provide similar built-in deterrents. We will discuss them later.

Second, reinforce yourself for delaying your reward. In Marcia's situation she might use self-praise to delay her museum trip until the end of the conference. Her self-statement could be, "Marcia, you're developing self-discipline. It's hard to stick it out but you're doing it." Be your own best friend.

If this sounds simple-minded, bear in mind that these ideas have a good track record. Put solid effort into them and you maximize opportunities for success.

When a change project simply doesn't work, the questions just addressed need to be dealt with. But if you *still* have trouble, don't nag yourself. If you do, you develop a negative association with trying. Simply shelve the project and go on to another. Build momentum through changing in other ways. Then if you return later, you might find you can manage the project after all because of increased confidence you have built along the way.

Watching Out for Mistaken Notions

The self-mothering idea of responsible reinforcement is not a simple panacea for any change. There are mistaken notions to be aware of.

NOT JUST ANY RESPONSE CAN BE CHANGED

It is self-evident that certain circumstances in our lives cannot be altered, and we must simply learn to live with them: height ("too tall" or "too short"), intelligence ("brainy" or "featherhead"), striking beauty (yes) or striking plainness, funny eyes (nose, teeth, neck, ears), a permanent physical or mental disability, terminal illness, divorce, the death of a loved one. Other circumstances may be less obvious but very real: a daughter raised in a family where a son is preferred, a husband who won't change with the times, elderly parents with growing infirmities, being raped, one's own personal aging.

Reinforcement, however, can help us *cope* with these unchangeables. Recognizing them, we can develop starter goals and target behaviors to live with the facts rather than wasting our energies in wishful thinking, worry, or feeling sorry for ourselves. Often this means living with and accepting the status quo; occasionally it means taking action so that we don't have to. Arranging for positive reinforcement for whichever of these paths seems best is something we *can* do. Then we can get on with our lives.

NOT ALL CHANGES REQUIRE
TANGIBLE REWARDS FIRST

Some people have the idea that tangible rewards are always stronger than intangible ones. Not so. Sincere approval from someone you love or admire, for example, is surely stronger than many tangible rewards people arrange for themselves.

Material rewards are needed only when others are not powerful enough. If you are intent on changing earlier socialization, your motivation may be so strong that intrinsic rewards carry you along with little or no additional help. These rewards come about first from realizing just what concrete actions you can take and second from your growing sense of personal control.

DESIRABLE ACTIONS ARE NOT
THE ONLY ONES REINFORCED

Reinforcement takes place continually all our lives. Women in our world are still reinforced for taking on the identity of the men they marry to the detriment of their own. Little girls continue to be rewarded by teachers and parents for being passive. By being labeled noncomplaining, older women are reinforced for not asking questions they deserve to know the answers to about health problems, banking, and old age benefits.

Reinforcement of what most of us consider poor behavior is frequently unintentional. A girl wears low-cut blouses to high school and receives reinforcing stares and comments from the boys. A wife, angry at her husband, won't speak to him for several days until he apologizes; his apology, in effect, rewarding her "silent treatment." A customer, breaking into tears when she complains to the male credit manager about her bill, has it quickly adjusted in her favor.

As women, we may unwittingly reinforce questionable behaviors in others. Kit, a young woman with large brown eyes and flaming red hair, approaches her office mates triumphantly. She has just walked her usual route to the office. It takes her past a building construction crew, and each day the hard-hats welcome her with whistles and catcalls. *Kit:* "Today as I walked by I finally had the courage to hold up my finger in an obscene gesture when they yelled at me. I had all I could stand. That showed 'em."

Showed them what? Kit's legitimate outrage nevertheless displays her vulnerability, thereby giving her tormentors encouragement. They are rewarded for their persistence and will figure in the future that if they keep the heckling up long enough they will again obtain a reaction.

If we are to take charge of our own lives, we must understand that all of us are constantly being "programmed" not just by planned but by unplanned reinforcement we receive or don't receive from people and events surrounding us.

Deliberately Reinforcing Others

SPECIAL REASONS WHY

To help others acknowledge our changes. We know that others close to us, including our children, invariably face adjustments in their own lives as we examine our socialization and gradually change our ways. For men it may be especially difficult.

Dan feels hurt because May no longer serves him beer

in the evening when he watches TV. She claims he is capable of getting it himself. Ken wishes his wife wouldn't insist on driving the car an equal time when they are on trips. He's nervous when someone else is at the wheel. Mike can't understand why Jane wants to go backpacking without him. He wonders if she still loves him.

It isn't only that we need to communicate what our needs are when we make changes, we also need to reinforce any efforts on the part of others to support us, fragmentary though those efforts may be.

"It really helps when you get your own beer, Dan. I love doing things for you spontaneously, but if I think you expect me to wait on you, I feel like a servant."

"Ken, it's a good feeling for me to know that you go along with my sharing the driving. It's probably not easy for you after doing all of it yourself for so long."

"I'm glad you're not uptight about my backpacking trip with the office group, Mike. I'll have lots to tell you when I get back."

Sara Benson (Chapter five) understands the importance of reinforcement for her husband, Richard, who deferred to her decision to take a real estate course. She lists ways she followed through:

1. After a class field trip to several homes, I asked Richard to return to one house with me to look at a specially shaped workbench that leaves room for a large vise on one side. We are now considering installing a similar one in our basement for Richard's workshop.

2. One evening Richard and I had a good talk about the values of houses, including ours, and he obviously relished the conversation. I offered some intelligent observations based on up-to-date data.

3. Richard must know I'm happier. I don't complain as much about mundane jobs in the house and with the children. That's a big payoff for the whole family.

To help others make changes of their own. Our reinforcement can support other women and encourage the men in our lives when they examine their own socialization and decide to make gender role changes. Furthermore, how we reinforce or do not reinforce our children's actions can release them from or tie them to their own socialized role patterns. Honest approval not only feels good, it does make a difference.

HOW TO REINFORCE OTHERS

Basic reinforcement rules apply equally to everyone. Beyond the basics, consider these points when dealing with others:

Be truthful. Recognize that which you really approve of, including tendencies toward improvement. Women socialized to please others are often astute at determining what other people *want* to hear and then voicing it, whether or not it is truthful. Don't risk losing precious credibility.

Routine "thanks" is weak. "Thanks" is sometimes only a little better than no reinforcement at all. Like superficial compliments, it is too often simply ritual, with true meaning lost. Much more reinforcing is a specific and relevant comment: "I finished on time as a result of your help. That meant a lot to me." Or, "I'm glad you encouraged me to follow through. I learned from that experience."

Be careful how you thank someone for helping you with a job you feel should be shared. For instance, Celia thanks Hank for putting the children to bed. She thinks this job should be divided equally, but by thanking him she implies that doing it is really *her* responsibility, not *theirs.* Celia would be wiser to describe to him how she feels. "While you put the kids to bed, I finally relaxed after a wild day at the office. Tomorrow I'll do it." Or after the children are asleep she might acknowledge (but only with honesty), "They really love your bedtime stories."

Use their rewards, not yours. Polly thinks she reinforces her boyfriend when she gives him attention, only to find that sometimes her attention is unwanted and occasionally even annoying to him. "I thought that since his attention always rewards me, mine would always reward him. But I guess not. He needs more time to himself than I do." It's easy to assume that what rewards us also rewards others.

Then, too, keep in mind that while just about all of us want approval from those that we respect, not everyone feels equally comfortable with praise per se. So even if you enjoy verbal recognition yourself, remember that as a way of showing approval it can be overdone.

Don't select a reward that raises inconsistent expectations. Darla's actions could give a mixed message: She shows her appreciation for her husband's sharing the clean-up of the dinner dishes by offering to pack his suitcase for a business trip. In so doing she is encouraging an equitable division of labor with reinforcement that fosters dependence and subservience. Her husband deserves appreciation but not by promoting expectations inconsistent with the reason she wants to reinforce him.

Be cautious about love or affection. If you say, "I really love you when you do that," or offer other affection, including sex, as a reward, the danger is that you imply that your love or affection will be withheld if the person does *not* respond as you wish. Surely it is acceptable to show your pleasure in a reinforcing way with a hand squeeze, a pat on the back, or eye contact, but remember that love should be constant, not used as a contingency based upon someone's actions.

Self-mothering extends to others because our own needs and desires are integrally tied to the needs of those around us. The spiraling effect of positive reinforcement creates better feelings all around.

Time for Yourself #12

For one week keep a record of ways you deliberately reinforce other people in your life for actions of theirs which you honestly approve of. Note their responses.

*Date   Honest Reinforcement I Gave Someone   Note Resulting
                                                Behavior*

CHAPTER SEVEN

Patterns from Others: The Power of Example

ROBIN: (Running out of her room) Mom! Come quick! There's a bug in here. It's wiggling toward me. Please kill it!

  MOM: Robin, did you know that being afraid of bugs is a gender-based stereotype of girls and women?

ROBIN: Then how come you aren't afraid of them?

  MOM: Because when I realized I didn't have to be that way I made myself get over it.

ROBIN: Oh. (Walking slowly back to room. Silence for 30 seconds.) SMASH. (The noise of a shoe stomping the floor.)

ROBIN: BLAUGH! Oh, gross! *I did it!* Please clean it up, Mom.

Rita is annoyed when she finds that the neighbor who admires her front-porch planter has bought one just like it. Adelle serves on a jury that decides a writer is guilty of quoting from someone else's material without receiving permission or giving credit. Ginny, aged nine, calls her brother a copycat for insisting on chicken noodle soup just because she asks for it.

People frown on imitators. Plagiarism is a legally punishable offense. "Copycat" is a jest resonating out of our childhoods. All the same, others' examples play a powerful part in shaping our lives, for they are a major way we learn.

IT CAN BE DELIBERATE

Teachers use modeling intentionally. As students we are asked to listen repeatedly to a French phrase, to watch how the tennis pro reaches for her serve, to observe the way the lab assistant pours from her vial. Then we are told to approximate the same actions.

Parents use modeling intentionally. Girls are told, "Sit quietly the way Shelly does." "Help your mother in the kitchen." "Trudi didn't get the car tonight, so why should you?"

Advertisers use modeling intentionally. Tantalizing women TV viewers by depicting an attractive woman with a handsome, attentive man, advertisers peddle cosmetics, cooking goods, and laundry detergents by suggesting that viewers, too, can be sought after and "successful" if they buy the recommended products.

IT CAN BE INCIDENTAL

As a way we learn, modeling is not only calculated but takes place without planning. Do you ever listen to a child speak in a language you don't understand and think to yourself how bright she is? Your reference point, of course, is your own native speech, acquired from incidental modeling of your parents ("mother tongue") and others in your culture, while the little girl learns her language by incidentally modeling the speech of people surrounding her.

Or take Phyllis. Fiftyish and farsighted, she wears bifocal glasses. When she buys groceries she has difficulty reading labels without tilting her head back to focus through the area of strongest magnification. One day in the supermarket she sees a woman using a pair of half-glasses with a stiff handle attached, the modern version of the old-fashioned lorgnette. Phyllis notices that with these glasses, little head-tilting is necessary, so she goes home and phones optical shops to locate a pair for herself. Without deliberately trying, she models another person.

Incidental modeling takes place with gender roles. As babies, our earliest identification is our sex. ("Is it a girl or a boy?") From that time on we gain approval when we model characteristics typical of our sex. We find common tendencies within each sex in ways we sit and stand and speak, do our hair, wear our clothes. Furthermore, we also model the interests, attitudes, and fears of our sex. For some children gender lines are quite rigid, almost black and white. ("Just girls get to use the oven." "Only boys play with shovels.") For others, more flexibility is acceptable. ("My dad is as good a cook as my mom." "Who says girls can't use shovels?") Incidental modeling constitutes the largest part of our hidden education.

IT CAN BE DESIRABLE OR UNDESIRABLE

Five-year-olds Joyce and Kelly, when they pretend they are mommies taking loving care of their baby dolls, demonstrate how girls model positive qualities associated with motherhood. Unfortunately, following the same female role models, Joyce and Kelly may also imitate self-limiting attitudes that encourage disinterest in things mechanical, putting themselves down, or acting helpless. At the beginning of this chapter, Robin probably modeled her mother's earlier fear of bugs, but now she takes her first step in the direction of her mother's newer autonomous attitude. (She might also model cleaning up the mess herself or removing the live bug to the outdoors instead of killing it.) Modeling results in a hodgepodge of personal actions, all of which shape the ways we act but only some of which are in our best interests.

Modeling for Self-Change

People often exercise no more choice over what they model than the proverbial monkey in "Monkey see, monkey do." How, then, does modeling become a tool for self-change? The answer lies in deliberately planning its use. **The Modeling Principle: To learn a new way of responding, observe a**

(prestigious) person who performs a behavior you want to learn and use that person as your example.

First of all, let's settle any hangups about copying. Virginia proclaims, "I don't want to be a clone. I want to be my own unique self." Well, Virginia, try as you will, you can never be completely unique, and you probably wouldn't like it if you were. Modeling is as inevitable as Santa Claus in December. Provided you think carefully before you decide what to model, you will find that you can benefit very well from someone else's example. Here is how to go about it.

SELECT CHARACTERISTICS, NOT TOTAL PERSONS

Model with a starter goal in mind, looking for the special qualities related to it in someone else's actions. We notice and learn from the way another woman handles sexist comments made in ignorance or how she takes credit for her own achievements in a nondeprecatory way. It is not wise, however, to try to imitate another person's total style, for we risk locking ourselves into their belief system rather than forming our own. Then Virginia's concern about being her own person does indeed become very real.

CONSIDER OTHER AGES, AND MEN

Because we identify most easily with people who are like us, it's often easiest to imitate persons of the same sex or about the same age. Keep your modeling options open. We learn from people who are different from us as well as similar.

Portia testifies to this. "My son, Chip, has long been a fan of John Lennon's. I never understood why and didn't bother to ask, assuming it was a generation difference. But when Lennon was assassinated, I read about him and was impressed with his ideals and what he meant to others, including my son. I wish I had allowed Chip's enthusiasm to capture mine." Portia regrets she didn't consider her son an example for herself.

In our society, unlike some others, the elderly are not as likely to be role models. Callie describes an exception. "Mrs. Farnsworth, a neighbor now in her mid-eighties, walks by our house regularly several times a week. Her destination is always the same. She is a regular volunteer at our nursing home—for the aged! She says assisting 'those old people' does more than anything else to help her retain an interest in life. I worry about growing old myself. Because of her I'm now volunteering with the English-As-a-Second-Language program. I want to stay involved with others as she does." Callie at age forty is modeling the actions of a woman more than twice her age.

Some women feel that deliberately trying to model a man is a cop-out. If the modeling is planned to learn a specific skill that a man possesses, why not? Gina (see next paragraph) may well find useful actions to model from her male executive peers. Provided she is selective, it does not follow that she will lose sight of her own special qualities.

MODEL BY USING YOUR IMAGINATION

At 37, Gina is the first woman in her organization promoted to a high management position. She will meet twice weekly with other executives, all older and all men. According to Gina, "I felt as if I had been suddenly thrust into a game without knowing the ground rules. How should I act?" With no female role models, she decides to imagine how she would ideally act. In her own mind she rehearses her role, beginning from the time she enters the conference room. But she finds this difficult. Next she thinks about how an imaginary woman executive might conduct herself, displaying her ability but being neither high-handed nor self-effacing. Finding this imagery more effective, Gina continues it in a more detailed way, imagining how the same anonymous woman cites facts, listens to others, and asks substantive (rather than logistical) questions. She then imagines the men treating her with comradely respect.

Imagination is a creative prop for modeling. Try it.

LABEL THE ACTION

You are in a group where several women laugh freely at a sexist joke. You talk with a middle-aged woman who will not allow her picture to be taken because she "looks old." You observe a father asking his teenage daughter to help serve a company meal while his teenage son continues to play. Let's say these incidents bother you. What can you do to help make sure you don't unintentionally model these persons yourself?

Immediately label. State clearly to yourself: "Don't act the same way!" "Don't imitate this!" Or simply, "No!"

Labeling helps us with actions we *want* to emulate as well. Perhaps you like how a woman talks back evenly and nondefensively when her point of view is attacked, or you admire a father who does not give in to his child's demands with company present. Then immediately label to yourself, "Great example!" "I like that!" "That's for me!"

BUILD IN REWARDS FOR YOURSELF

When modeling works it is because we feel good about the results. If built-in rewards aren't sufficient, try thinking one up, as Gina does when she wisely imagines comradely approval for her actions in the executive meetings.

Time for Yourself #13

Select a starter goal and look for specific examples of it modeled by people you observe in your everyday life. Deliberately practice imitating one of these examples, using it as a target behavior for yourself. Reward your efforts.

Sources of Modeling

To use modeling advantageously rather than to become innocent victims of its misuse, we need to be well informed about who our potential models are.

PRESTIGIOUS PEOPLE

How satisfying it is to believe we are becoming more like the special people we look up to. Role models having the greatest impact on us are those whom we admire.

People who are famous. Movie and TV stars, athletes, scientists, and people holding public office all illustrate the kinds of famous personalities whose actions we imitate. Through the years, modeling accounts for Princess Diana hairdos, the increase in face-lifts after Betty Ford announced hers, and Mark Spitz mustaches in the mid-1970s following his multiple Olympic championships.

People you know. For role models we often pick persons in our everyday lives, especially those we like and respect: a teacher, a friend, the woman down the street who seems to have her life all together, a favorite aunt.

Annette is a stockbroker in her mid-forties. She fought hard for her present position and is not sympathetic to other women who complain how tough it is in a "man's world." "I grew up wanting to be like my aunt. She stayed single, held a responsible job in a publishing company, wore clothes nicer than anything my mother owned, and took vacations to places that sounded glamorous—Hawaii, Spain, the Grand Canyon. I remember how she shocked people by saying that she loved money—loved to make it and loved to spend it. To me she was stylish and strong, an individualist much like the fictional character Auntie Mame. I really didn't feel the pressure to find a husband while I was in college as so many of my friends did. I wanted to find work to support myself in the style of living I admired in my aunt's life."

For Annette, her aunt dispelled a fear held by women in her generation of "ending up an old maid" and contributed to a fiercely competitive spirit that gained Annette success in the male-dominated world of investments.

When Gretchen spends time with her college roommate and boyfriend she notices that they both freely admit when they are wrong. "They don't make a big issue out of it, but it impresses me because they don't try to cover up their mistakes with each other." Gretchen, who says she has difficulty admitting her own errors to anyone, decides to make the effort to be more open about them with her own boyfriend. Her roommate is her model.

Women often unintentionally imitate the men in their lives, since the greater power represented by men in traditional relationships increases their prestige:

COLLEEN: I never thought about why I drive in the fast lane on the freeway until someone asked me. George always does it, and I guess when I began driving I automatically did the same thing.

DANA: Since Todd never worries about whether the children eat balanced meals, I find I'm much more inclined now to let them eat whatever they want at mealtime.

MELANIE: Howie has been a football nut since before we were married. Now I'm hooked, too.

Mom and Dad in particular. Our parents deserve special mention. Usually they are, of course, our first role models. Combining (we hope) authority with nurturance, they also enjoy prestige. Whether our admiration continues depends on many things, including how reinforcing or punitive they are and how our other role models regard them. But one thing is clear: We are highly vulnerable to the examples they set.

"One thing I really admire about my dad," says Erica, "is his ability to express his opinion without hurting others. I've often heard him say that he feels honesty is imperative, but that a person also needs to be socially responsible for its effect on others. I've really tried to watch how he puts this into action. He uses discretion and stays constructive, and part of it is that he couches his honesty in a quiet, nonthreatening manner. It's an art and not easy to learn, but I try to be this way with my friends, and I really think it helps."

Belle is shaken when her brother says to her, "You know what's wrong with you? You criticize people just like Mother does." They think their mother finds fault with everyone. Is it possible that she, Belle, is doing the same thing? Yes, it is quite possible. In contrast, Francie describes her long-divorced mother as a survivor. "She's been through a lot but is a real fighter. I felt really complimented when my uncle told me I'm tough just as she is." That's also possible.

Charles M. Schulz

GRANDMOTHERS CAN BE GOOD ROLE MODELS, TOO

Child abuse can be perpetuated from one generation to the next through modeling. Parents, not liking the way they themselves were treated as children, may nonetheless imitate the same harshness with their own children, and be inadvertently reinforced by the built-in (though temporary) satisfying release of their own anger.

Many, many contributions parents and also grandparents make to their children, both favorable and unfavorable, are the direct result of modeling.

114

ANYONE YOU HAPPEN TO NOTICE

Ann pushes her way through the Christmas shoppers toward the front entrance of a major New York department store. She is to meet her husband in twenty minutes and is early. With time remaining, she pauses at a jewelry counter to view some watches, then leans over to get a better look.

"Get your arms off the counter, lady." The intrusive command comes from a tired salesperson with dark circles under her eyes, growling after a day's abuses from a mass of humanity. Ann, surprised, immediately straightens up but finds she is unable to read the price of a watch she has spotted. "The one on the bottom shelf with the red strap. How much is it, please?" she asks.

"The same price as the one just like it with the white strap up here in front of you," responds the salesperson, pointing but making no further effort. Ann draws back, intimidated but angry, and ponders how a person can possibly deal with this woman and not lose.

She looks on with empathy as a second shopper is told sternly by the clerk to take her package off the counter. Then a third woman appears, looks intently at several display cases, and signals the salesperson. Ann prepares for a verbal onslaught as the shopper asks to see two watches from different cases. The salesperson takes out just one and places it on the counter. "And now the other, please," the woman asks. "How much is it?" The clerk ignores her.

For a moment the shopper continues to examine the watch she is given. Then, gaining eye contact with the salesperson, she says evenly and with a smile, "You must be very tired from working here by the door all day in the Christmas rush so I'm sure it is easy to get annoyed when customers ask questions, but I do need to see the other watch and to know how much it costs so I can compare them."

At this point the clerk's demeanor changes, and Ann detects embarrassment. "Oh, of course," she says. A few minutes later, after examining both watches, the shopper hands the watches back, thanks the clerk for showing them to her, and leaves.

Remaining polite, reflecting the other person's state of

mind, pointing out in a face-saving way its impact on others, and finally repeating what she wants (and why) now becomes part of Ann's own repertory. While it doesn't always elicit such a positive reaction, she still finds it useful. Her deliberate modeling all started with a chance encounter.

PEOPLE ON TELEVISION

The idea that crime on TV is imitated by certain people who see it on the tube and then commit bizarre crimes in real life you will recognize, of course, as modeling.

We hear much less about television's stereotypic images of women and men—in commercials, soap operas, and prime-time programs—and how these portrayals serve as examples for viewers. Reruns, both old and not so old, are often flagrant grounds for criticism. But even today, TV writers and advertisers, imagining life as they themselves have known it, perpetuate gender stereotypes. The main difference is that stereotypes in new programming are less obvious. If we view TV passively, we simply won't recognize many of the sex-typed actions portrayed and often condoned before our very eyes—actions we may imitate without realizing it.

To understand the full range of TV modeling possibilities, try a deliberate double-take method of viewing. Cue yourself not only to look once at the obvious message but to look back again quickly. The second time check out gender stereotyping. Only then should you decide what you want to model and, equally important, what you don't. At that time immediately label the action according to your decision.

To assist your double-takes, specific questions such as those below are the kind to ask yourself about a female portrayed on TV:

When she is viewed in the home, is she involved with activities in addition to domestic tasks (instead of being shown holding a coffee pot, cleaning the floor, or wearing an apron)?

Is she portrayed primarily for her looks (and as "pleasing the guys") or does she possess unique personality characteristics (and a concern for the larger issues of life)?

Does she have a warm, noncompetitive relationship with another woman?

116

Does she make her own decisions or is she told what to do and if so, by whom? Do males ever seek her out for advice?

Do commercials portray a woman advertising anything other than products for home use and beauty preparation? Is a woman viewer made to feel guilty if her home and family's clothes are not spotless?

Let these questions, pointing up potential negative or positive modeling influences from watching television, inspire others of your own.

Time for Yourself #14

With the above questions in mind, plus those of your own choosing, select and observe a variety of TV programming—prime time, re-runs, soap operas, and commercials—and take notes on positive and negative role models for women in each.

Men as well as women suffer from gender stereotyping on TV. We see men portrayed as "strong" when they are controlling and unemotional, or bumbling and misunderstood when portraying the father role. A husband is often domestically dependent for his personal needs. To understand stereotyping of females we need to be on the lookout for it in men's and children's portrayals as well as our own. We live in the same world: Our roles are interdependent.

PEOPLE YOU READ ABOUT

Nor does modeling stop with people we observe. Another abundant source is people we read about.

You probably know that nonsexist guidelines now exist for school texts, but they do not affect many books you read as a child, have in your home, purchase over the counter, or that you take from the library. Like TV reruns, gender-biased books are easily accessible. Therefore, responsibility for "de-stereotyping" our reading and for recognizing potential negative and positive role models will continue to fall on us as individuals.

The double-take method of viewing TV applies equally to reading. In fact, when you consider labeling the actions of a woman or someone else you read about sometimes the same questions can be asked. Here are a few others to generate more ideas.

Is she described mainly as a "helper" or also as an innovator and a "do-er"?

Is she portrayed with fears that she allows to limit her actions or that she faces up to and copes with?

If she asks for help, is it primarily from males?

Is a mother described spending time on activities devoted to her own growth in addition to helping her family?

How often is a woman depicted in a career other than teaching, nursing, or secretarial work?

Encourage the children in your life to hunt for gender bias and to label the actions of potential role models they read about. Nine-year-old Vicky describes it this way: "It's like that game in kids' magazines where you look hard at a picture and try to find things hidden in the drawing, things you can't see at first, like an elephant, an umbrella, or a clock. Sometimes you have to look very carefully to find something, but it's neat when you do." And even neater if adults show enthusiasm and share observations.

For older children and adults, a variety of books about positive women role models exists. Biographies depict female pioneers, economists, scientists, writers, and artists. In addition to the occupations, many of these offer modeling ideas for dealing with gender issues that are equal to any you will find elsewhere.

Newspapers are our handiest modeling source. Here women are coming into their own: career stories about women telephone installers, politicians, sportswriters, symphony conductors, auto mechanics, professional volunteers; stories about women with unique occupations, such as a teller of Indian legends, a woman founding an agency to handle odd jobs, another organizing a directory for free and inexpensive goods; life-style stories about combining motherhood with full-time paid work, not being trapped into husband's work as a conversational ornament, successfully avoiding dependency on grown children. These articles have special impact because they are fresh, newsworthy examples of women right now and are often loaded with modeling ideas. Similar articles appear in the top magazines treating women's issues.

MYTH: A DEARTH OF ROLE MODELS

We hear a lot about a lack of female role models. How can this be when women represent more than 50 percent of the population? Female role models abound. Of course, that's the trouble, for most of our would-be role models are caught in the same binds we are. They model the same old responses, or if they don't they agonize over perplexities strikingly similar to our own. They may well model their concerns, but they often don't model solutions.

Another myth: the so-called Superwoman. Talk to almost any Superwoman when her hair is down, and she will level with you about the juggling of schedules, the lack of sleep, the guilt about not spending enough time with her children, possible worry about outshining her husband, not having the time to enjoy her big salary, and how the glamour is exaggerated.

One celebrity, a movie star known as a superb actress as well as a political crusader, when asked how she was able to combine these roles with motherhood said first,

"You really need to be well-organized."

"But do you ever wonder if it's all worth it?"

"Well, you have to plan very carefully."

"Even so, isn't it terribly difficult at times?"

"Okay. . . . It's hell."

Women who have found solutions are few, and their answers are highly individualized to fit their own situations (a grandmother as baby-sitter, a showcase executive with a baby crib in her corporate office, a boyfriend who is a feminist, a woman whose work can be performed at home, a husband whose hobby is cooking). We say these women have it made. But they have problems, too.

Here we are, then, surrounded by women role models, many of whom are examples of the status quo and are looking

119

for their own solutions, and a few who appear to have made it but are not always sure of that themselves. These women are all potential role models. But sometimes when we imitate them without realizing it, we compound our confusion. To model successfully, stay alert, be deliberate, and remain highly selective.

CHAPTER EIGHT

Advance Notices: Alerting Yourself to Cues

Dear Abby: I'm 19, work in a large office and people tell me I'm pretty and have a nice personality. I never have any trouble getting dates, but here's my problem. All the guys think I'm "hot stuff." Maybe the fact that I measure 39–26–36 has something to do with it, but I can't help it. I am definitely NOT hot stuff. I am very picky when it comes to guys, and nobody gets a thing off me, but they all try it on the very first date. What's wrong with me? I want guys to respect me, but this "hot stuff" label defeats me before I have a chance to prove it's not true.

Hot Stuff

Dear Hot: Check your packaging. Do you wear "come hither" clothes? Check your language. Do you tease without realizing it? And finally, check the look in your eyes. Nobody has ever made a pass at a statue.*

*Taken from the Dear Abby column. San Francisco Chronicle, Sept. 16, 1977. Copyright, 1977, Universal Press Syndicate. Reprinted with permission. All rights reserved.

Subliminal advertising, the notion that TV flashes suggestions about products to viewers without their being aware of it, thereby influencing their buying habits, stirs public cries of mind control. Yet every day we are all influenced by untold numbers of undetected signals prompting various actions. Not only do we react to these cues, we elicit them as well. Abby points this out when she asks Hot Stuff to check her packaging. She is telling her to check out the cues about herself that she may unknowingly give others.

Sources of Signals

Most cues in our surroundings come from several identifiable sources. Let's look at these sources and see how various women respond to the cues.

PERSON CUES

Someone said women act "one hundred and eighty degrees differently with men than with other women. It isn't just the men who do the game playing." Aroused by this, Yvonne and Alice decide to monitor their own actions.

YVONNE: I find I make my own decisions except when there is a man around. Then I wait for him to make up his mind—anything from when we eat to how to spend my own money. If I don't agree, I acquiesce. In building up men's egos, I'm wondering what I've done to my own.

ALICE: I'm finding I don't like to compete with men. Ever. But I sure like to take on other women. You could say I compete selectively.

We are cued to many of our actions by the particular people around us due to the impact of such factors as age, past experiences, or, as with Yvonne and Alice, gender issues.

PLACE CUES

The way we act in a barber shop is quite different from the way we act in a beauty parlor. Or contrast how you behave in your own home as compared to a place of worship, a swanky dress shop, or a singles bar. (Imagine men's locker-room dialogues compared to their dinner-party conversation.) *Where* we are surely suggests certain behaviors. In other words, we use "place cues."

"A woman's place is in the home," the ultimate gender place cue from past generations, reflects how much our thinking has been shaped by a place cue that women until recently seldom questioned.

Paula cues herself to attend German class by parking her bike early in front of the classroom door. Then she walks to a nearby coffee shop with friends, more confident that she won't be tempted to ignore her class later on. Paula arranges a place cue to work for her.

TIME CUES

Jenny and Lori have a little more personal power because they recognize time cues they put to work for themselves.

Asking herself when she most often squanders her money, Jenny determines that it is just after she picks up her paycheck, for at that time she often shops impulsively. As a result, she asks to have her paychecks mailed directly to her bank rather than to receive them at her office.

"I've heard the song often, but this time it was played for the last dance at a party," Lori said. "My date told me to listen carefully to the words as we danced. The lyrics went, 'Lady, lay down beside me.'* A cue, of course, but not the way he expected. In this case, it kept me on guard the rest of the evening."

CUES FROM WITHIN

Self-prophecy cues. A few women are actually so self-assured that the positive self-prophecy cues they give themselves both reflect and create personal confidence. They are the ones who say with candor, "I get along well with both

---

*From "Lady Lay Down," a country song by Rafe Vanhoy and Don Cook, © 1978 Tree Publishing Co., Inc. and Cross Keys Publishing Company.

women and men." "I learn easily. Studying is no problem for me." "I expect to be at the top of my field in twenty years." These women appear to belie their socialization. They are exceptions.

Most of us identify more quickly with negative self-prophecy cues that program us *not* to succeed and actually hold us back. Do any of these sound familiar?

> "I won't ever be able to get up and talk in front of a group."
> "This (mistake) proves I'm incompetent."
> "I'll never balance this checkbook."
> "I don't have any control over what happens anyway."
> "I know I'll never have an orgasm during intercourse."
> "I just can't do this all alone."
> "I'll never have the figure I want to have."
> "I'm not pretty enough to make a good impression."

Women making statements like these can and do change. Stopping negative self-prophecy cues is not all that difficult once we understand we're really sabotaging ourselves. (More on self-sabotage in Chapter thirteen.)

Body cues. We know about body cues for thirst, hunger, elimination, and sex. And we have trained ourselves to notice body cues (symptoms) associated with fear and stress. Physical signs also tip us off to feelings of hurt, anger, fatigue, or guilt. Yet we may dismiss these signals, not realizing they can serve as critical cues to help us deal with our feelings.

Eleanor cleans her house for weekend visitors. "The problem is that everything comes at once. Not only do I need to clean, I need to make beds and prepare meals. But my back! It really gets to my lower back." Eventually Eleanor is forced to bed for a week to recuperate from sciatica. She is learning the hard way not to ignore body cues.

Lola says she was an easy touch when a certain woman acquaintance would ask her for all-too-frequent favors (to care for a child after school, to copy a recipe she wanted, to share fund-raising jobs). "When she would phone me asking for help, my stomach would be in knots. I'd say yes and then feel angry. But now when she phones and I get that sensation in my stomach, it reminds me that my body is sending out its own alert. I use it as a cue to delay a reply: 'I'll call you back.' Then I think it over first. Sometimes I still say yes, but when I decide to say no I also rehearse in advance how to tell her."

The inner signals our bodies give us are really languages of their own—both the private thoughts and the body sensations. Learn to tune in to them.

CUES FROM ANTICIPATED CONSEQUENCES

Positive expectations. "Jus' 'fore Christmas I'm as good as I can be." James Whitcomb Riley's children's poem points out how positive expectations cue us to certain actions. Roxanne, for example, tells the man she goes out with that she is 39 rather than 45, anticipating that he will find her more desirable. And Meredith, expecting to maintain a high credit rating, makes certain her bills are paid promptly each month. Both Roxanne and Meredith are cued to certain actions due to anticipated positive results.

Negative expectations. Two years ago Janie was the victim of an attempted rape. Immediately afterward she took steps to ensure her own safety: She and her husband moved into a more secure apartment and put special locks on their door, she completed a course on the use of mace, and she made certain she did not walk alone anywhere at night. But that's not all. Now she will not stay on any elevator unless there are several people in it, daytimes she will leave her car in a garage only if an attendant parks it for her, night-times she relies on her husband to take her to and from her business meetings. He also does the grocery shopping, either with her or by himself. Although she complains about how these self-imposed measures have sharply restricted her life style (to say nothing of her husband's), she does not question whether she might do anything differently. She is determined to avoid all situations in which there is even the remotest possibility of an attack.

There is also Georgette, who suffered through an un-wanted pregnancy. She now tries to avoid intercourse with her husband to prevent becoming pregnant again. "We get

along, but our sex life is twentieth-century Pompeii—dead."
And there is Kitty, who is terribly hurt because her long-time
boyfriend jilted her. Kitty shies away from other potentially
meaningful relationships with men for fear she will be hurt
again. Janie, Georgette, and Kitty continue to shun situations
because of negative expectations resulting from earlier experiences.

Avoidance holds built-in rewards. When Janie continues
to withdraw from all possible situations where she might be
attacked, she is encouraged to do so by the security she feels
in not having to face up to any risks, however remote. (She
also receives strong, reinforcing consideration from her husband.) Similarly, for Georgette and Kitty avoidance means they
do not run the risk of pregnancy or rejection. Partly because
of the built-in comfort accompanying avoidance, it is often
difficult to end. If you suspect you are avoiding, ask yourself
appropriate questions: Am I restricting my life (or the life of
others) more than necessary? How else might I face this issue?
Am I withdrawing because I might be hurt? Should I encourage
myself to risk a little? And not least, what rewards am I
receiving because I avoid? If your answers suggest changes
you want to make, use them as cues to devise starter goals.

CUES FROM COMBINATIONS

Often more than one cue signals our actions. Liz breaks up
with Mark, her live-in boyfriend of two years. It is an amicable
parting, and they continue to see each other frequently. But
Liz complains of difficulty breaking off their sexual relationship
even though she claims she wants to do so. Let's take her at
her word. As she monitors the circumstances surrounding her
liaisons with Mark, Liz finds they always take place in the
evenings at her apartment. "Then he ends up spending the
night." If Liz really wants to stop having sex with Mark, she
could begin by changing the cues—that is, meeting him in
the daytime and away from her apartment.

Cues in our environment are like the setting of a play
in which you are the major actress. In real life, know what
cues set the stage for your own actions. The structural diary
(Chapter three) helps you identify them.

Signaling Your Own Self-Change

The Cueing Principle: To strengthen or develop a new action, note the situational cues immediately preceding the present action and change them to other conditions that prompt the behavior you desire. Not only can we make the surrounding cues we've just discussed work for us, we can develop cues of our own.

SELF-INSTRUCTION CUEING

In self-instruction cueing we become our own coach. One way to do this is deliberately to use our own feelings or actions as cues for the changes we want to make:

> "I feel hurt. This is the time for me to reevaluate."
> "I'm a motor mouth! Get others talking."
> "I'm tired. This is my cue to change what I'm doing."
> "I'm getting a lot of ideas from others. Now what are my own?"
> "I'm controlling too much. Better let up."
> "I'm being overly ingratiating. Be more honest."
> "This situation will continue until I take action. Get started."
> "I'm beginning to sulk. Keep communication lines open."
> "I'm encouraging sexist behavior. Stop giggling."

We also cue ourselves to action with simple direction-giving. In Margaret Mitchell's *Gone With the Wind,* Scarlett O'Hara's famous "I'll think about it tomorrow" is an example. Here are others:

> "Establish eye contact. Shake hands firmly."
> "Don't lay on the guilt."
> "Listen very carefully to this conversation."
> "Don't be coy."
> "I'm not going to let myself withdraw from the situation."
> "This is a legitimate time to put myself first."
> "Don't expect people to act the way others want them to."
> "I will now firmly remove his hand from my knee."

We can give ourselves cues for larger tasks, too, as if we were reading a recipe or responding to directions on a questionnaire. Natalie in her first supervisory job describes how: "I still prompt myself privately when I give orders. 'Don't forget: Make it simple and direct. Be clear. No more than one please or thank you. No tentative questions. Ask for feedback. Remember, you are in charge.'"

Although giving instructions out loud to yourself isn't generally feasible, when you can do so you will find you may remember them longer. The "hearing" sticks in your head.

THOUGHT–STOPPING

Sometimes before we can give ourselves input we first need to rid ourselves of nonproductive, intrusive thoughts and self-put-downs (often negative self-prophecies) that we can't seem to kick. A special kind of cueing called thought-stopping* helps. Here is how it works.

When an intrusive thought keeps reoccurring ("I can't stop thinking about him"), or when you talk to yourself in a deprecating manner, sharply say, "STOP!" If possible say it out loud. You might clap your hands together at the same time. Jolt yourself. Wake yourself up. Get your attention. Then immediately substitute a relevant positive thought in its place. ("*Stop!* He isn't the only guy in the world.") Do not permit yourself to get by with the notion buzzing around in your head. Become your own policewoman.

In addition to coping with self-defeating statements, situations in which women have found thought-stopping helpful include the ending of a love affair, mulling over problems only others can solve, the effect of aging on one's looks, and the death of someone close.

Pay attention to intrusive thoughts when you first encounter them to see under what conditions they persist, or as in the death of a loved one to allow sufficient time for grief to run its course first. Then when you do try thought-stopping, stick to it awhile if you expect it to work. It's not a total solution, but it can help.

*Joseph Wolpe, *Psychotherapy by Reciprocal Inhibition*. Stanford, CA: Stanford Press, 1958.

CUEING WITH IMAGERY

By imagining scenes, we can cue ourselves to improve our performance. "Put it this way." "Hold that until later." "This sounds okay." "That's better." It is, once again, a use of rehearsal.

Some people write out an imagined script to cue themselves. Priscilla finds that her own version of scripting cues her to greater efficiency when she phones a busy person. In advance of the call she frames the questions she wants to ask and writes them down in what she imagines will be the logical sequence of the conversation. *Priscilla:* "This cuts down on my tendency toward verbal overkill and leaves a better impression."

AUTOMATED SELF–CUEING

If you need a memory jogger, cueing can be wordless as well as automatic. Marylee places her airplane ticket in her jewelry box because she knows she will open the box to pack her earrings. Leslie, wanting to lose weight, puts the bathroom scales in front of her refrigerator. Greta leaves on the TV set her skirt that needs to be hemmed to remind herself to sew it while she watches the news.

And not least, Caroline. Caroline now realizes that although she's been told she is the "greatest mother figure around," she has not yet learned to take care of herself. "It's important to me to help others. I don't want to change that. But now I've got a new system. Each time I notice myself giving affection to someone else, I deliberately nurture myself about something. It's my cue to indulge myself a little." That's using the head as well as the heart.

Time for Yourself #15

Read over again the self-cueing methods just discussed and within the next week apply each of them to target behaviors of your own.

In self-change, there are two reasons to learn about cueing others: to become aware of cues we give others unknowingly and to become skilled at judging when it is acceptable to cue others deliberately and then to do it in a way that is least likely to be offensive.

CUEING OTHERS WITHOUT NAGGING

The *American Heritage Dictionary* defines a nag as a person, *especially a woman,* [author's italics] who pesters or annoys by constant scolding, complaining, or urging. Let's not perpetuate another female stereotype. To make certain we understand the difference between cueing and nagging, here are guidelines for verbal cueing:

Cue prior to the desired action, not afterward. Recalling the verbal cueing game of Simon Says helps us remember this. It is never "Simon told you so." Anything said afterward is not a cue, for it is a reminder of what should have been done rather than signaling what to do. Tell someone in advance, "I'm going to need a few minutes to myself now" rather than saying afterwards, "Why didn't you leave me alone?"

Be diplomatic. Make the cue pleasant, presenting it under calm conditions, rather than shouting, "Go away! Don't disturb me! Can't you see I want to be left to myself?"

Be clear. Our own ambiguity can destroy our purpose. If we say, "I'm going outside" when we really mean we need to be alone and don't want others tagging along, we may encourage misunderstanding. Be as specific as possible.

Use verbal cues sparingly. Being repetitious places us somewhere between naggers and whiners. The antagonism created often makes further verbal cueing impossible. When cueing doesn't promote the desired response, stop. Look for another method.

Melinda is married to an architect who recently started working for a new firm. They have two daughters, two and four years old. Jeremy comes home each evening exhausted from the strain of his new job, but Melinda has to deal with an adjustment of her own. A former nurse, she finds that the confinement of staying home with two young children is "making me climb the walls. I badly need more outside life, but we're barely making ends meet financially, and I don't know people to trade baby-sitting with. I'm stuck except for times Jeremy is home on weekends. I'd like to get together with a teacher friend on Saturdays, but that requires help from Jeremy with the kids."

Jeremy, however, makes his own plans. When Friday comes it is his cue to plan his weekend relaxation, and he does. To quote Melinda: "Jeremy announces each Friday when he plans to play racquetball the next day and arranges his weekly errands around it. Result? I spend another day with the kids."

Melinda tries simple verbal cueing, incorporating the guidelines just mentioned. One evening early in the week when the children are asleep and their life is peaceful, she says, "Jer, let's discuss how we can work out baby-sitting for next Saturday so that you can get in your racquetball and I can meet Sandy for lunch. I badly need some time away from the kids." They then discuss dividing up Saturday's baby-sitting.

Melinda is on the right track. She picks a comfortable time to talk. She is diplomatic. She asks Jeremy before he makes his own plans. She is clear about what she wants. Afterward Jeremy feels good about pleasing her. To establish a new pattern, she will want to follow up in future weeks.

Melinda's original situation illustrates a problem common to many women—failure to communicate their own desires clearly enough. Open communication is often overlooked as the best way to do this. Melinda's open communication is couched carefully with verbal cueing to promote success. If it doesn't work, she would be better off trying other ways rather than risk nagging, which only damages further communication.

AUTOMATED CUEING OF OTHERS

Given the possible negative side effects of verbal cueing, this alternative can prove useful.

Mary Ellen, a reentry student with school-age children of her own, devises several automated cues to help her family know when she is busy studying and when she is free. The cues to her availability are when her study door is open, when she answers the phone, and when she is visible in other parts of the house. They know they can always interrupt in an emergency. She also has a note on her study door saying, "Before you knock, will it wait until my next break?" (That note is not an effective cue over time, but it helps to begin a new way of thinking for potential knockers.)

Doing nothing sometimes becomes an automatic cue. Many women complain that they wish their families would pick up after themselves more often. Since traditionally women have taken responsibility for the appearance of the home, many of us are ourselves cued by the sight of messiness, and we immediately step in to clean up—putting away children's toys strewn on the floor and men's socks not tossed in the hamper. Those sights spur us to action, but *our* actions cue others *not* to take the responsibility, since they find that if they do nothing these tasks are performed anyway. If you want your family to understand that you are not running a personal maid service, don't become a personal maid.

Once upon a time there was a young woman of unsurpassed beauty. No one could avoid noticing how lovely she was. When friends yearned for more attention from men, they would inevitably remark to her, "But you don't ever have to worry about that. You just don't know how lucky you are." In one way it was true. She did not worry about being attractive. Hers was the opposite problem. How could she describe to friends the agonies of being looked over, stared at, whistled at, followed, and the object of talk wherever she went? How could she describe the fear she held that people would not like her for herself but only for her beauty? How could she be certain a man loved her for herself alone? How could she explain what a terrible burden she considered her looks to be without sounding ungrateful? She felt she could not, so she learned to keep silent.

To cope, she devised her own automatic cueing method. She covered her spectacular figure with old, loose, ill-fitting clothes. She allowed her hair to cover part of her face, then combed it as little as possible. To her tried and true childhood friends she was still her old self, but to others she was sending

out another message: "I'm just a plain person; let me be."
Beautiful women can have problems, too.

Automated cueing of others can be mechanical. A Scottish scientist developed a birth control device that is an electronic bra. It flashes a red or green light to indicate "when it is safe to have sex with a woman wearing it."* (We would prefer that the computer tracking her ovulation period signal the woman to make her own decision.)

CUEING THROUGH TRY–OUT ROLES

With others actively participating, role-playing and reversing of roles give participants practice in cueing others about their needs and feelings. Imagine acting out various rejoinders to these situations women have confronted:

- How to respond, if pregnant, when a man says sincerely, "I understand if a woman looks beautiful it's supposed to be a boy. You look beautiful."
- How to respond when someone asks you to be on a committee "because we don't have a woman in the group" rather than for your great ideas.
- How to respond at a cocktail party when a stranger opens a conversation with, "Do you do anything?"
- How to respond when you invite a man to a business meal and he grabs the check, saying, "I insist. It's not every day a chick invites me to lunch."

Practice in combining diplomacy with an enlightened response gives us more confidence for cueing others. Find a friend and try cueing through role-playing. It's not only instructive, it's fun.

ANTICIPATORY CUEING OF OTHERS

Jessica, separated from her husband, receives a letter from him saying he would like to meet her for a weekend in Aspen, Colorado, an easy drive from both of their homes. Purpose?

---

*By permission of United Press International, *San Francisco Chronicle,* February 20, 1979.

To discuss their marriage. Jessica is ambivalent. On the one hand, she feels it would clear the air to talk; on the other, she knows he would like to get back together and she does not want him to assume she is ready to do so. Therefore, in her answering letter she states her feelings, saying she will come provided they have separate accommodations. Now he knows well in advance what to expect and can plan accordingly.

Hank phones Lara to go to the movies. "I'd love to if I can be back by eleven," she says. Hank is cued in advance to her curfew and will not be upset being told during the evening instead.

Before they marry, couples ordinarily talk over their expectations for the future. In a casual way this is anticipatory cueing. But with so many more life-style options today, fewer assumptions can be made as to what a woman or a man expects to receive or to give in a relationship. More structured anticipatory cueing helps couples understand each other's expectations and prevents later problems. Here are selected questions to elicit long-range anticipatory cues for dual career couples planning life together:

1. How many children, if any, would you like to have? What is your opinion of various birth control methods? Of abortion? When would we plan to have children?

2. What are your ideas about how children should be raised? How much time do you think children should have with their mother? Their father? How would this affect the employment of either parent?

3. Under what circumstances would the following chores be assumed or shared: handling income taxes, preparing meals, washing dishes, grocery shopping, getting car repaired, cleaning house, changing children's diapers, getting up at night with the children, staying with sick children, chauffeuring them (to school, extra lessons, friend's houses, physicians, dentists, etc.)?

4. How important is it to you to have a picked-up or clean house?

5. If one of us needs further training, how could this be worked out fairly for the other person?

6. Under what circumstances would you be willing to move if an excellent job opportunity came along for me?

7. What do you think would be an equitable arrangement for our finances?

8. To what extent would you expect me to participate in the socializing aspects of your job—e.g., entertaining or being entertained by clients, visiting VIPs, the boss, etc.? What role would you expect me to play (bartender, cook, companion, best friend, room fixture, you name it)?

9. How would you feel if I earned more money than you or had more demands from my job (e.g., travel)? Would you feel competitive, threatened, willing to arrange your time to help with my schedule?

10. What issues might we place in a contract that could be renegotiated after a given period of time?

11. Do you believe in monogamy in marriage? How does this relate to each partner? To work separations? To separate vacations?

12. What interests do we have in common that we can pursue together? Do you enjoy or mind spending time alone? How important is companionship and under what circumstances?

This list is not complete. Couples add items of their own. Long-range anticipatory cueing is intended to stimulate thinking about the future of the relationship so that each person knows in advance as many needs and desires of the other as possible. It suggests a flexible, rather than a set, pattern to follow and prompts clearer communication.

FOLLOWING UP WITH OTHERS

The other half of cueing others, especially to our own needs, is follow-up reinforcement when people accommodate us. With cueing, low-key recognition may be more gratifying than flashy kudos.

CUEING OTHERS
IN THE WRONG DIRECTION

If others sometimes "get the wrong idea about us," here are some misleading cues women may accidentally give that can help explain why.

Misleading cues due to gender role expectations. Sandra complains that Kenny, her boyfriend, always makes the decisions about what they will do, with whom, and when. But from the time they first started going together, whenever he asked her opinion on such matters she responded with, "Well,

I don't know," "Whatever you like," or "I don't care." She thereby cued Kenny to be the decision-maker in their relationship.

When two people are close, each tends over time to assume certain roles. Before we cue partners to react differently, we should ask ourselves whether our own behavior cues them to their present actions.

Elaine recently took a position as a college teacher in a campus community where she knows the wives and children of many of her colleagues. She is eager to establish herself professionally. Walking down the hall, she greets one colleague and asks about his wife, discusses the children's new piano teacher with another who drops by her office, and one day before a departmental committee meeting when a friend's husband, who is also Elaine's colleague, speaks to her about washing-machine problems at home, it dawns on her what is wrong. She is giving the wrong signals. Until her professional credibility is well established, she would be better off sticking to academic issues at school and saving social topics for social occasions.

Margo is a mother who complains because her family relies on her too much. "They never give me any time for myself." But Margo is also the mother who sends her children elaborate gift packages when they are away from home, suggests that she make their doctors' appointments for them, and tells her husband he is in the way when he tries to help in the kitchen. Margo cues her family to depend on her but resents their doing so.

Misleading cues due to our speech. Regina, an interior decorator, phones her client. "Do you suppose it might be possible for you to drop by, say, a few minutes later, maybe, let's see, at four thirty instead of four?" Patty, a junior college student, scribbles a note to her teacher: "I'd sort of like to have this paper back later. May I please come by to pick it up sometime at your convenience?"

Under the guise of politeness, Regina and Patty word their questions in such a way that each comes across as tentative and wishy-washy. Instead of asking a simple question such as, "Is it possible for you to come at four thirty instead

136

of four?" or "I would like to have this paper back. When can I pick it up?" each complicates her request. This kind of speech leads to ambiguity ("Just what does she want, anyway?" "Get to the point!"). It also suggests that the questioner is unsure of herself. The cues are ones of weakness.

Misleading cues due to our appearance. It is almost like a cult—if three people can be a cult. Three first-year college women are always identifiable in their dorm as the local overall freaks. Not just ordinary overalls. Each has a pair that is spray-painted enough to look like a New York subway train. They wear them almost constantly and seem to love the extra attention they receive. Except for one thing. Although the male students enjoy them as casual friends, they don't seek them out for romance.

Griping one day to an older student about the lack of "interested" men on the campus, the three are asked in response, "What kind of vibes are you sending out? Funny vibes? Old-joke vibes? Wear-the-same-crazy-clothes-every-day vibes? Are these the signals you give if you want some guy to look twice?" These women are told that their attention-getting antics turn men away from serious interest. On the other hand, Dear Abby suspects that Hot Stuff, the nineteen-year-old whose letter appears at the beginning of the chapter, may have the opposite problem. ("Do you wear 'come hither' clothes?") Whether we like to think so or not, our appearance inevitably makes a statement about us that is a cue to others.

Misleading cues due to our body language. Abby also suggests that Hot Stuff check the look in her eye. She's referring to body language cueing. Here is another example.

Tammy is furious. "You won't believe what happened last night. Listen to this." Over lunch Tammy relates to two women friends the saga of her first date with a new man. "And at the end of the evening he tried to get me in bed with him. When I said absolutely not, he blew up and said I had been leading him on the whole time. I can't believe it." Tammy's indignation is echoed by her friends. They each feel a little vicarious violation. During the remainder of their meal Tammy's friends ask her detailed questions. Here are excerpts of their conversation:

"Where did you sit when you got into his car?"

"Sort of in the middle of the front seat."

"Did you hold hands at the dance?"

"Sure, who doesn't?"

"Did you slow-dance?"

"Of course. Why not?"

"What did you do afterward?"

"We listened to records."

"Where?"

"In his studio?"

"Was there a bed? Did you sit on it?"

"Yes, there was. No, of course not. I sat on the floor."

"How did you sit?"

"Have you ever sat up rigidly on the floor for very long?"

"How did you sit?"

"Well, I leaned back on the floor."

"Where did he first kiss you?"

"In the car."

"When?"

"After the dance."

"How long did that go on?"

"Well, we were there for maybe, oh, I don't know, twenty minutes. Now listen, it really wasn't the way you're thinking."

Sometimes body language speaks louder than words. Tammy claims she really liked her date and simply wanted him to know it, but her cues misled him, suggesting she was willing to go all the way. When rebuked, he became angry.

We all use body language: A wink, a kiss, a squeeze of the hand, a raised eyebrow, a frown, a pout, the way we stand. They each send their own messages.

Responding to Others' Signals

We know that our own actions cue others to a number of different responses. When the situation is reversed and others cue *us*, how do we react? Do we ignore our own needs? Are there times when unwittingly we relinquish control so that "being acted upon" is a logical consequence? If you think this is possible, here are some suggestions:

Label the signals others give you. Say to yourself, "He wants me to do this." "She expects me to take action." "They don't want me to say anything right now." "Society expects this of me." This alerts you to the fact that you are receiving cues, just as the labeling we discussed in Chapter five alerts you to role models depicted in reading or on television.

Ask yourself whether you have received the correct cue. One mother, aroused by her fifteen-year-old daughter's complaints about a salesperson, said she would call the store, whereupon the daughter declared, "I'm asking you to be a listener, not to fight my cause." The mother had misjudged the cue.

After labeling, cue yourself to make your own decision about what to do. Cues do not necessarily require action, but when you choose to do nothing (deliberate nonaction), act out of conviction and not because you wish to avoid making up your mind.

Recheck your response to others' signals. Do you feel a sense of control? If you don't, reexamine the previous three points.

As with fears, cues from our environment control us unless we learn to recognize them. When we do, we can exercise increased personal control by responding more deliberately to the signals we receive and by learning how best to devise our own.

Part 4

DISCARDING HABITS THAT SLOW YOU DOWN

Do you notice habits that seem to discourage even your best efforts to change and grow? Chapters nine and ten describe ways in which planning excesses and ignoring responses can slow up and even stop habits you don't like. In Chapter eleven you will look at an important way to combine ending a response with substituting something better. If you wonder about using punishment as a way to stop habits, you will think twice after reading Chapter twelve, but nevertheless you will learn how to time mild aversiveness for positive results. Finally in Chapter thirteen you will see how women may unintentionally sabotage their own best efforts and what to do about it.

Read about all of the methods first before deciding which are the best for a specific action you want to stop. Not all methods are equally appropriate or desirable.

CHAPTER NINE

Curbing Responses Through Planned Excesses

> What this office needs is a soundproof room
> where you can blow your top.
>
> Roberta

> ⠆ attribute my success as an editor to boredom.
> The four walls, the diaper pails, the soap operas—yes,
> and the whining little kids tugging at my skirt. It was
> so awful to me that I simply had to do something. For
> me, leaving all that behind was my great motivator.
> Becoming a newspaperwoman was a means,
> not an end in itself.
>
> Hanna

"John Jacob Jingleheimer Smith" is an old campfire song. Its words repeat themselves in such a way that there is no ending. You sing it until you tire of it and finally, somewhere along in the nonstop melody, fatigue or boredom sets in. You simply stop. When Gale says, "I've had it up to here discussing sexism with Mary Jo" and then motions with her hand under her chin to indicate where "here" is, we know she is sick of thinking about it—bored. Shirley states emphatically, "No chocolate chip cookies for me. I ate too many one time. You know what

it's like to toss your cookies? Well, I can't stand them now."
These are all examples of satiation. Here are others.

Wendy's husband, Matt, insists on helping prepare the
evening meal. Being naive about cooking, Matt asks many
questions and performs each job so slowly that Wendy, who
first was eager for him to share the work, becomes disenchanted. "He's sweet, but he drives me crazy asking all those
questions. It takes forever. I'd rather do it alone." Wendy is
fed up with her cooking partner.

Job burnout is a term used to describe negative reactions
people have to their work due to exhaustion or boredom. It
is accompanied by lowered performance and the worker's
admission that she or he would do just about anything to
change how the work time is spent. The person is disinter-
ested, worn out by the job.

Although we usually think of burnout in connection with
office jobs, it can happen with home chores too, as Hanna
describes above. Connie's aunt is another example. Her Aunt
Bertha was well-known as a gourmet cook whose meals Connie
remembers from childhood. Returning as an adult to visit her
aunt's home near Chicago, Connie remembers those sump-
tuous meals from the good old days. When her aunt asks her,
"What would you like for dinner, chicken or ham?" Connie
selects chicken, whereupon her aunt suggests going for a walk.
It leads them to the local grocery store where they buy a
whole fresh chicken and take it home. There Aunt Bertha
places it in a pot of boiling water. One hour later, stabbing
it with a fork, her aunt lets it slide onto a platter saying,
"Connie-girl, I'm tired of fancy meals; this is just as healthy.
Now help yourself."

Connie: "That boiled chicken wasn't just the entrée. It
was the entire meal. Boiled chicken with salt and pepper."
Apparently Aunt Bertha's gourmet meals became more of a
chore than a pleasure, resulting in job burnout.

When excesses from consumption or activity occur, we
want to stop. To overcome this feeling we alter our actions—
end the singing, change the subject, stop eating the cookies,
or look for a way to vary or discontinue the job. It happens
to all of us. It is a part of life.

Applying Satiation
to Stop Your Actions

By deliberately using satiation we can also stop actions that we simply don't want to continue but that are not that easy to change. **The Satiation Principle: To stop a certain action, allow or insist that the behavior continue until fatigue or boredom sets in to end it.** After you see how other women apply this principle, read about the cautions concerning its use and ways to combine it with other methods before trying it yourself.

As a device to stop certain habits of your own, satiation can be useful under some conditions you will already recognize.

HOW MANY PEOPLE ARE BECOMING SATIATED?

Drawing by Booth; © 1978
The New Yorker Magazine, Inc.

BOOTH

"Mrs. Van Lewis-Smythe, third wife of your chairman of the board, said to me this evening at the corporate hoodingy, and twenty people within earshot, 'We all know what Mr. Parmalee does. He is a very important vice-president of the Hi Lee Lolly Corporation. What we are all wondering, Mrs. Parmalee, is . . . just what is it that <u>you</u> do? Do you do anything?' I said, 'Mrs. Van Lewis-Smythe, Your Grace, I fix dripping faucets around our house. I prop up sagging bookshelves. I glue broken china. I clean windows, mirrors, floors, walls, pots and pans, and dishes. I jiggle the doodads on running toilets. I repair and refinish furniture. I cane chairs. I paint and sew. I do electrical work, drive nails, saw boards, and I give birth to our babies. I wash and iron and make the beds. I prepare the meals. I get the children to school. I trim the hedge, plant and maintain a vegetable garden and flower garden. I mow the lawn, clean the basement, feed the birds, the cats, a dog, and a chicken, <u>and</u> I chauffeur a very important vice-president of the Hi Lee Lolly Corporation to and from the bar car every blessed day.'"

VENTING PENT-UP FEELINGS

Bottled-up emotions can be released without hurting others if we use satiation wisely.

Andrea, angry at her boyfriend for betraying a confidence, goes into the bedroom, locks the door, screams into her pillow and hits its angrily, then cries until she is exhausted. After that she feels better, for the same reason that Roberta half-jokingly advocates a private sound-proof closet to let off steam in her pressure-filled office situation. If you can find your own place to vent your anger harmlessly or to cry your eyes out, you are using satiation as an aid to rid yourself of pent-up feelings.

Total absorption in some form of creative expression until we "run out of steam" is a way others give vent to their feelings. You will recall that Anais Nin, the diarist mentioned in Chapter three, wrote to express and sort out her own strong feelings as a woman. If you haven't tried this method to come to better terms with your private world, you may wish to. You don't need to win literary prizes before you do.

The following letter to Ann Landers* illustrates an application of satiation to help overcome sorrow at the end of a love affair.

Dear Ann Landers:

I read somewhere (I think it was *Us* magazine) an article on how to get over a collapsed love affair. Please pass it on.

The basic theory was that most victims fail to overcome their sorrow because they don't suffer enough. These people should have what is called a "Grief Olympics." It should start immediately after the affair is over. The grieving should last a full 24 hours.

The broken-hearted one should gather all the gifts, letters, pictures and anything connected with the former beloved and put them well out of sight. Next

*By permission of Field Newspaper Syndicate, *San Francisco Chronicle and Examiner,* February 10, 1980.

146

the sad soul should indulge in an 18-hour agony orgy that will in the end set him free. The advice was—cry your eyes out. Don't use the phone. Don't see anyone. The mourning must be done in solitude. Also, it stressed—no fancy food. Just cottage cheese and water. Play sad music and suffer. After awhile exhaustion will set in—then boredom.

When the Grief Olympics have been completed, it is important to make new friends. Do not avoid the old haunts once enjoyed with the former beloved. Go there with a new acquaintance. It worked for me and I recommend it to others.

Ann G.

Dear G.:

The piece did indeed appear in *Us* magazine. It was written by Candi MacConaugh. The "therapy" was designed by Dr. Zev Wanderer, a UCLA lecturer who treated heartbreak cases for 13 years, but confessed he never realized how painful rejection by a lover could be until it happened to him. I would not endorse the Agony Orgy for everyone; however, different strokes for different folks.

We agree with Ann Landers that such extreme methods are surely not for everyone, but the letter does illustrate how deliberately satiating feelings can help some people more quickly end the agonies of a broken romance.

STOPPING EXCESSIVE HABITS

Beth works on a starter goal. Given to extravagant apologizing, she decides on two ways to satiate herself to stop the habit. First she practices overapologizing by herself repeatedly. "I'm sorry. Really I am. Oh, how can you ever forgive me? Wait. I have more to say. I just want you to know I feel terrible about this. Really I do. I'm really sorry. I feel awful about it. Oh, golly, this is terrible. I'm so sorry. I'm so-o-o-o sorry."

Second, Beth asks a friend to reverse roles and apologize profusely to her. Beth's conclusion: "Well, it sure didn't take long to find out how others must feel hearing those repeated apologies, even though we exaggerated and didn't always remain serious. We still kiddingly break into these ridiculous routines whenever an apology arises, but actually I've learned my lesson: Apologize once and stop."

Having been told she complains too much about how she feels, Judi sits down by herself in front of a mirror and tries satiation: "I feel yucky today. I'm so tired. Not enough sleep. Head feels woozy. I expect a sore throat. Exhausted. That's me. Exhausted. Oh-h-h geez, I just can't get going. I'm worn out." *Judi:* "I got so tired just talking about being tired that I eventually quit in disgust." Nevertheless, Judi will need to use this method on additional occasions when she complains if it is to be a valuable deterrent over time.

Denise has a gimmick of her own. Her starter goal is to stop using obscene language, and her satiation method is to tape-record herself talking with all the picturesque speech she can muster. "I've played that tape about a dozen times to myself. At first I was embarrassed, then I laughed. Next I noticed how limited my dirty vocabulary really is. Now I really dislike listening to it. It's boring. Although I still use some of the words now and then, I sure don't use them as often. They're trite."

Carefully combining satiation with certain other principles can increase its effectiveness. Trish's starter goal is to stop using so many male-based phrases in her own conversation. She combines satiation with cueing. When she finds herself saying "Oh boy oh boy oh boy," it cues her to follow up with "Man alive," "To each his own," "Far out, man," and "Oh, brother." Each time she runs out of ideas, she wraps it up with "Peace on earth and goodwill to all you folks out there."

Similarly, Louise wants to stop using self-descriptive sentences containing certain words. "When I hear myself saying 'I *must* . . .' 'I really *should* . . .' or 'I *ought* to do this,' I repeat and enlarge on those sentences emphasizing the key words. To myself of course. But I also make certain I give myself credit when I remember to use the 'I wants' and 'I prefers.' This helps me not to ignore my own needs, and that's something I should, I mean I *wish* I'd done for years." Louise combines satiation of one action with rewarding another, an excellent way to start a new response at the same time stopping one you don't like.

In order that you not become satiated with examples, try on your own to apply satiation to these habits other women wanted to stop: declining with many excuses, overjustifying reasons when making a mistake, and nagging to get someone to take action.

IDENTIFYING HABITUAL ERRORS

To correct a simple but habitual error with satiation you may practice it deliberately before trying to change it.

Eve uses this method when she finds herself consistently punching keys in the wrong sequence on her computer. She identifies her incorrect fingering and deliberately repeats it several times. (It helps to label it "wrong" in your head, too.) This way Eve becomes completely aware of what the mistake is. She then practices it correctly (labeling it "correct").

People find this method of identifying habitual errors helpful as an aid for correcting misspelled words, improperly remembered names and phone numbers, and even spooner-isms. ("I'll be in the larking pot. *Larking pot.* L-arking p-ot. L-arking p-ot. Okay: *parking lot.* Parking lot.")

REMOVING BLOCKS IN THINKING

Writing nonstop—not even lifting your hand from the paper—helps to overcome the paralysis some of us have when we try to write carefully constructed ideas for others to read. It helps break down the personal criticism that prevents writers from recording their ideas freely. When no thoughts come, filling in with any nonsense or repetition helps stop the self-censoring. If you have this writing problem, try "free writing."

(An oral version for people in groups is "brainstorming." Participants are given a problem to be solved and instructed to call out any solution that spins through their heads, however outlandish. Without restrictions, blocks to thinking are less-ened and ideas—both crazy and serious—begin to flow, encouraged by free association, until no more are forthcoming. From this motley assortment several plausible solutions are selected for closer scrutiny.)

ENDING AVOIDANCE

Occasionally by our own contrivance we can immerse ourselves in an activity previously feared and avoided and learn to cope with it. Myra wants to stop being so concerned about driving on freeways. She is a competent driver but always prefers circuitous, time-consuming routes to avoid using them. When she finds a beautiful apartment down the freeway from her job, she realizes she finally needs to face up to freeway driving if she is to move. She decides to try it. "This will force me to change my attitude if anything will," says Myra, and she rents the apartment. After only one week of the forced daily commute, she is reasonably comfortable with the freeway even though she had avoided it for years.

Note that Myra doesn't apply a hierarchy such as we describe in Chapter five in order to cope with this fear. She faces it head on, motivated by a new apartment that is more important to her than clinging to her old behavior. Her work doesn't permit her to arrange driving times around a hierarchy so she simply plunges in—sink or swim—knowing she wants very much to succeed. Already an experienced driver, she finds that total immersion in freeway driving dispels her old concerns. Satiating her driving discomfort, she brings her avoidance to an end.

Applying a hierarchy is a much safer way to overcome fears, but when conditions are right, facing up to a situation through total immersion may help you put an end to it. Nevertheless, do not consider using this method with large fears without professional assistance.

Applying Satiation
to Stop Others' Actions

Lois uses satiation to fend off an argument. Her husband, Cliff, returns home for dinner after work. Lately he is increasingly critical of her meals, and their usual open communication is strained.

CLIFF: Broccoli *again?*
LOIS: (*evenly*) Anything else wrong?
CLIFF: You made too much today. I'm tired of it.
LOIS: (*evenly again*) What else don't you like?
CLIFF: Dinner isn't ready either.
LOIS: (*evenly, if it kills her*) Anything else?
CLIFF: Well, how long will it be until we eat?
LOIS: (*hanging in there*) What else?
CLIFF: I'm tired. I've had a rough day.

At this point when Cliff stops nagging, Lois wisely responds immediately to his change in a sympathetic and positive way, although she claims it is not easy.

By dealing with his nagging through low-key but insistent questioning (satiation) Lois hopes to end Cliff's crankiness and make her point, at the same time not encouraging a big scene. When she reinforces his self-disclosure about fatigue, their communication is off to a better start and a larger argument is avoided.

Some women will object to the temporary deprecation Lois puts up with, but she claims she feels a continued sense of control. Her persistent low-level questioning not only quickly wears down her complainer but serves as a cue for him to change, ending further unpleasantness. Some men will say Cliff's reaction is not typical, that logically he would be more resistive. In that case both of them might be contributing further to their breakdown in communication.

Using satiation this way does counter another's actions toward you, but it has risks. It worked for Lois and Cliff probably because of her low-key approach, but its quality of insistence can quickly put people on the defensive and damage a relationship.

Simply allowing a person's actions to continue until the end comes about naturally, holds more appeal for most of us even though it often requires our conscious restraint. Take a mother who decides to put up with a harmless though annoying teenage fad (hair-style, clothes, speech, music). She may well be more successful encouraging its demise if she lets it "play itself out" rather than making an issue of it and running the risk of reinforcing a behavior that would then continue longer.

Cautions About Satiation

CONTINUING A BEHAVIOR
MAY BE HARMFUL

Before you consider ending any action with satiation, ask yourself whether prolonging it holds any dangers. Obviously, deliberate, excessive use of alcohol or other drugs is no way to stop such a habit. And logic dictates that Lois will surely damage her relationship with Cliff if she uses her confrontive style of questioning on many other occasions when he complains, even though it was successful once.

CONTINUING A BEHAVIOR
MAY BE REINFORCING

If the action itself is reinforcing, satiation will not take place. A danger exists by stopping too soon and allowing positive reinforcement to occur. Some women think that bingeing will satiate their desire to overeat. But bingeing contains the built-in reinforcement of eating itself, and unless a woman binges until she becomes ill and no longer can stand the sight of food each time, it is rewarding more than satiating.

Women have been known to attempt satiation with obscene phone calls from men. "Anything else?" "Would you repeat that?" "What else do you want to say?" "Go over that again." "What?" "Once again." Their objective is to exhaust the caller, to satiate him so he'll hang up. But the risk is that the caller will receive reinforcement to continue to mouth obscenities instead. The woman may respond with anger or fright in her voice, thereby encouraging the caller, or he may have others around to cheer him on. It is not a wise way to deal with crank calls. (In Chapter ten we will discuss a safer alternative.)

Janine and her roommate think they can satiate their sloppy housekeeping by being as messy as possible in their dorm room. They reason that when they finally clean up it will be such a relief that it will be much easier to stay neat from then on. So they deliberately hang their clothes on chairs, the chandelier, and the bedposts, as well as leaving them all over the floor. The effect is so striking that people walking by inevitably make comments: "How often do you change the display?" "Are you having a rummage sale?" "Did the clothesline break?" "Is this the Goodwill receiving room?" With such unexpected attention their sloppiness is an uncluttered success. Why change?

Applying satiation requires common sense. It is not the only way to stop responses and often not the best. But once in a while it applies so neatly to a situation that you will want to keep it in mind.

Time for Yourself #16

Having read the cautions about the use of satiation, select a suitable starter goal and apply satiation to help stop a habit of your own.

CHAPTER TEN

A Woman's Privilege: Declining to Respond

> I didn't answer when Mike asked who would take notes. Eventually he did.
>
> Renée

> I had a crush on Eric but I finally gave up. He never paid any attention to me.
>
> Cindy

Sit down with two friends for a few minutes and take turns with this game:

Person #1 tells a very funny or a very sad story about three-minutes long. It can be something that happened to her recently or something she read in the paper or saw on TV. But it must be funny or sad. She tells the story to person #2, whose task is to listen minimally without eliciting positive or negative responses either by what she says or how she acts. In other words, person #2 tries not to react either in her speech or in her body language to the story person #1 tells. Person #3 sits to one side. Her job is to observe person #2 and, if necessary, quietly point out to her any reaction she unintentionally gives to the story-teller. Person #3 remains as inconspicuous as possible, not participating in any other way, whether with eye contact, laughter, or groans. After about three minutes the story-teller stops and each person expresses her reactions to the "non"-response of person #2. Person #2 reciprocates by describing how she felt in her role. Then the roles are alternated.

Surely a situation admittedly contrived to be humorous or unhappy makes it more difficult than otherwise not to express the expected reactions, but dealing with extremes allows us a sharpened perspective in order to make two important points.

The first point concerns the difficulty most of us have when we try not to give any reaction, either negative or positive. To give a neutral, or what we call a "non"-response, requires self-control. Sometimes lots of it. How do you perform as a nonreactive listener? Do you give any positive cues you are unaware of? Can you manage being neutral without being negative? Some people feel that women, socialized to be sensitive to others' feelings, have more trouble with neutral reactions than men do because we feel we *must* be responsive. In any case, non-response is something that everyone can learn with practice (and with feedback from a knowledgeable friend). This chapter explains why this skill is important. Once developed it will come in handy many times.

The second point concerns how it feels when others do not react to us and what we do as a result. As the story-teller, how do you feel? Most people say they are uncomfortable, push more and possibly exaggerate to make a point, or seek responses from other sources such as person #3, but just about all claim that without some display of interest they don't want to continue very long. A non-response typically makes people work harder for a while to try to force a reaction that isn't there. But the end result, given no peripheral encouragement, is to stop trying.

Like satiation, extinction is very much a part of life. We recognize it when Cindy gives up her crush on Eric because he consistently pays no attention to her, or when a sign in a store window signifies lack of interest from customers: "Bankruptcy Sale. We quit." We ourselves unintentionally extinguish positive actions, and how we do this is described shortly. But first we'll see how extinction can work *for* us; that is, to stop habits we *don't* want continued.

Applying Extinction
to Stop Your Own Actions

The Extinction Principle: To stop a certain action, make sure no rewards follow it. Using extinction with ourselves involves looking at the world around us in a special way. We search into all the reaches of our surroundings and ferret out any hidden rewards that perpetuate the behavior we want to stop. Sometimes this is not easy because the rewards are well concealed. But once we find them, our challenge is one of changing the circumstances somehow so that rewards no longer exist or are minimized.

REARRANGING YOUR SURROUNDINGS

Meryl, a chemist, reports on her trip to a science meeting in Boston:

> I'm really a bookworm. I enjoy working by myself and am pretty shy when it comes to meeting people. My Boston meeting was important partly because I needed to make contacts in my field. I went there knowing no one and feeling uncomfortable about getting acquainted.
>
> The format of this meeting was a one-hour presentation, a half-hour break, and an hour discussion period each half day. Usually under such circumstances I take off during the break for an enjoyable solitary cup of coffee. However, this time I reasoned that a trip to the coffee shop was really rewarding myself for *not* meeting others. So I decided to stick around after the first presentation, even if I didn't circulate. Sitting there reading program notes was not at all as reinforcing as going off for a hot cup of coffee by myself.
>
> In the afternoon I again did not allow myself a private coffee break. By this time the program notes were boring, and when someone nearby struck up a conversation about the presentations, I finally began to change from remaining aloof to becoming a part of that meeting. I began to get involved.

Meryl followed the maxim, "Don't reward yourself with an activity you especially enjoy (coffee) when by doing so you avoid an activity you want to increase (making contacts)."

Emily, a single parent, returns home tired after a day's work. Changing into her night clothes and lying on the sofa to watch TV after an early supper is a source of much pleasure. In fact, her comfort is so great that she finds it difficult to struggle forth after the seven o'clock news to tend to household chores and most of all, to make clear to her children, ages twelve and fifteen, that she is available. "Obviously, it's wonderful to snuggle up on the sofa and relax with an evening of TV after a busy day," says Emily, "but at this point in my life I can ill afford to."

Her starter goal is to stop watching TV after the news unless there is a special program. Aware of her present rewards gained from casually relaxing all evening, Emily rearranges her routine so she no longer changes into night clothes after dinner, and she watches the evening news sitting up. "Not as pleasant, that's for sure, but if it were pleasant, it would be hard to get up and turn off the TV."

Both Meryl and Emily rearrange their circumstances so that rewards for former habits are minimized. But notice also how other principles in conjunction with extinction helped these women. Rewarding conversation initiated by another person turns Meryl from her solitude toward active participation. Emily employs self-cueing (by remaining dressed and sitting rather than reclining) to keep herself going after the evening news. It would help her further if she could also arrange rewards for her new habits.

PREVAILING ON OTHERS

Try asking other people to help you extinguish personal responses you want to stop. You are still the one in control.

Julie: "I never pass up a chance to make some deprecatory joke about my appearance or clumsiness. I want to stop it." Julie appeals to her good friend Coco for help, saying, "Don't respond when I make these jokes about myself because just about any reaction at all rewards me. Do absolutely nothing." To be most effective, not only does Coco need to remain neutral but so do others as well. Otherwise Julie may stop joking in front of Coco but continue when others are around.

Cheryl's problem is similar. She too realizes how much she degrades herself. "But," she says, "when I say things like 'I really don't know what I'm doing,' 'I can't do that,' or 'I give up,' I find these remarks elicit encouraging reactions from my family like 'Oh, c'mon. We know you're smart. You can do it.' " Recognizing the positive feedback her self-deprecating comments elicit, Cheryl cautions her family *not* to respond to her when she talks that way.

Cheryl and Julie might add in their instructions to others that they would welcome encouragement at *other* times, but not right after they put themselves down. It's a matter of timing.

Yvette freely admits her anti-male statements are encouraged by her apartment mates. When she decides she wants to stop making these remarks she involves them, too. She asks first that they give her absolutely no response any time she makes an anti-male remark, and second, that they make no anti-male comments in front of her because, she explains, she finds it difficult not to imitate them. The others finally agree. Since their actions are so ingrained, their first attempts at not responding to Yvette produce uncontrolled laughter, but gradually they react less. Yvette reports that not only did her own derogatory remarks diminish, but so did those of her friends.

UNINTENTIONALLY EXTINGUISHING
YOUR OWN BEHAVIOR

"It's no fun anymore," says Mazie, accustomed to daily early-morning jogging sessions with her husband, Gene. So Mazie no longer jogs and hasn't since Gene gave it up due to a knee injury. Mazie's rewards for jogging are based on companionship with the man in her life rather than the jogging itself.

With some trepidation, Nell speaks up at a PTA meeting about the number of junk foods in the school lunch program.

It is not easy for her to talk in public but this time she manages to do so. After she finishes, silence prevails, and no one responds to what she says. Finally the chairperson suggests proceeding to another topic. The next time Nell feels strongly about an issue in a meeting she does not voice her opinion.

If Nell were accustomed to talking publicly, one such occurrence with no reactions would not make her stop speaking up. But when a behavior is not well established, it is more easily extinguished. No wonder she opts not to speak the next time.

Congratulate yourself when you recognize that extinction is likely to end a behavior you really want to continue. Then you can rearrange your surroundings so that you receive some sort of payoff to keep it going. For example, Mazie might seek another running companion, or Nell might arrange in advance for others to back up her opinions at the meetings.

Applying Extinction to Stop Others' Actions

Open communication is the time-honored way to resolve problems in interpersonal relationships. Holding our own with others by speaking up and expressing our rights more fully is championed by the assertion movement to help assure that we receive fair treatment. However, there are times when openly saying how we feel or otherwise asserting ourselves to stop others' actions that affect us seems either inappropriate or insufficient. Another possibility is to use extinction; but we need to understand first how it works with others and what the cautions are.

IGNORING ACTIONS COMPLETELY

You have used the extinction principle with others without knowing it, perhaps when not responding to men's whistles or to your child's demands for attention, hoping that by "not hearing" the noise it would stop. We all know the cliché, "Ignore it and it will go away."

159

As Evan dangles a dead grasshopper by its leg in front of her face, Dawn remains undaunted and says calmly, "When you remove that insect, I can see what I'm doing." At a meeting where she was the only woman, Renée says later, "I didn't answer when Mike asked who would take notes. Eventually he did." April continues to talk uninterruptedly when someone calls to her to answer the phone. "I was busy. She wasn't. I didn't want to be used." Holly looks ahead and doesn't respond when the boy next to her whispers something about the plot in the movie they are watching together. Turning back to the screen, the boy does not continue his interruption. These are all instances of neutral or non-responses to others.

Then we have Elisa, a waitress who confronts a brash, bumptious customer at her lunch counter. *Elisa:* "At first I laughed nervously when he talked to me, and I also must have looked uncomfortable. (I was.) But since he still got a reaction from my embarrassment his heckling continued.

"Then I wised up. One day when he came in he began hassling me as usual, trying to get to me, but I simply paid no attention. It was *very* hard to do. The next time he came in I didn't even look up, and someone else took his order. From then on I continued to ignore his comments completely. He's gradually stopped teasing, but for a while there it was awful."

Until Elisa recognized that she might unwittingly have been encouraging this man, she didn't try to control her own reactions. But when she consistently offered him no attention, he persisted for awhile and then gave up. Some people would say Elisa's response was more negative than neutral, but she maintains "I was not snotty. I just kept busy so I didn't have to give him the time of day."

Elizabeth, a widow in her mid-seventies, has a close friend who is also a widow. But when her children come to visit, Elizabeth likes to go out to dinner with them alone. "I just couldn't tell Helen openly that she wasn't welcome to come along, but she kept hinting. Since I really didn't know what else to do on several occasions, I simply ignored her hinting and kept talking about other things. She finally stopped." Not realizing it, by ignoring her friend Elizabeth was using extinction successfully.

To use a truly neutral response, remember that both verbal and body language should suggest neither support nor hurtfulness. One woman terms it "flat affect." After trying the exercise at the beginning of the chapter, you know it takes practice.

REACTING MINIMALLY

In everyday life, giving no response at all is indeed difficult and often impossible. Then, too, some women are uncomfortable not responding at all because it seems impolite at times and therefore not neutral but negative. These objections are less serious with the minimal response.

When people do react but only at the lowest possible level, extinction may still work. We notice this when a person responds not negatively but with the least amount of enthusiasm or with ambiguity: "Maybe so." "Perhaps." This "vagueing out," noncommittal reaction includes keeping your *SUDS* level intact. When the minimal response is maintained consistently, its effect, though seemingly dull and uninspired, is often stronger than you might think.

Joy's father-in-law, William, pressures her about her husband Bert's career. While she wants to remain on good terms with Bert's father and understands the legitimacy of his concern, she does not want to encourage his efforts to use her as an intermediary to help subvert Bert's own career interests. She tries the minimal response:

WILLIAM: Surely you are aware, Joy, of the strange hours Bert must keep in his job. Isn't that going to be difficult in the years ahead?

JOY: (*Evenly, with minimal feeling*) Perhaps.

WILLIAM: Well, don't you think it would be wise to get him interested in something more stable, with regular hours?

JOY: (*Slowly, with little enthusiasm*) It's hard to say.

WILLIAM: My own company would take him on as a trainee, you know. He could have a brilliant future. What do you think?

JOY: (*without joy*) I don't know.

WILLIAM: You really should talk to him. He needs to understand these things.

JOY: (*ambiguously*) Maybe so.

WILLIAM: Talk to him, Joy. He listens to you.

JOY: (*low key, but politely*) Perhaps.

Joy makes no promises. She speaks without eagerness, passively. Remaining well-mannered, she attempts to convey a message of neutrality. If instead she projects interest or eagerness, she will reinforce William's strong opinions. Her choice of responses is as important as her demeanor. (Sometimes people respond with an "uh-huh" response, thinking it is noncommittal, only to find that the other person interprets it as "I'm hearing you" or "I agree," which is positively reinforcing, not neutral.)

Joy will probably have other encounters with her father-in-law on this subject. Maintaining consistency in her reactions over time is necessary if she is to end his pressuring. For now she prefers to establish a holding pattern rather than either confronting her father-in-law openly in disagreement or allowing herself to be talked into something she doesn't really go along with.

Alison receives three crank phone calls during a three-night period. The person at the other end doesn't talk but breathes heavily. When the fourth call comes at a predictably late hour, Alison is prepared. She picks up the receiver, places it on the table quietly, and leaves it until at a much later time (certain that the breather has hung up), she replaces the phone on its hook. After three more attempts, followed by her minimal response over several nights' time, the crank calls end. If they did not, she would have notified the phone company to take action.

Alison's solution is an alternative to no response at all (not even picking up the phone). We consider this method of handling crank calls far less risky than using satiation, although it is not foolproof, because the caller may still receive reinforcement from other sources.

EXTINGUISHING OTHERS AND REMAINING SUPPORTIVE

Grace assists a young scientist from a foreign country to become settled in their community for a year. She invites him to family dinners, drives him on errands, and helps him buy his groceries. When she realizes he now *expects* her assistance, she gradually stops giving him so much attention. However, she continues to talk with him by phone and arranges to meet him occasionally for tea. With her decreased accessibility he becomes more independent and broadens his friendships.

Sometimes people think that extinguishing another's response automatically signifies a broader lack of support. Grace's continued contacts with her new friend illustrate that this need not be the case.

We also are supportive when we help to extinguish the guilt and hurt that a person experiences from failing. Whether that person is a subordinate, a spouse, a child, or even ourselves, it is all too easy to rub it in in order to make certain the lesson is learned. But an "I told you so" message punishes the person still further. In contrast, minimally recognizing or even ignoring the failure helps lessen or extinguish negative feelings associated with it. After all, guilt and hurt are poor motivators for improvement. Helping to end them allows the person to regain self-esteem, a much sounder basis for positive change.

COMBINING EXTINCTION
WITH OTHER PRINCIPLES

For years Sadie Mason, 74, services her Studebaker at a gas station near her apartment. Shortly after a change of ownership at the station she pulls in to buy gas. The new owner is a tanned, muscular young man in his early thirties whom she has never seen before. He swivels around to her window and as she rolls it down says, "Hi ya, sweetheart. How about some gas?"

Sadie is stunned. Two generations not only in age but in personal style separate them. Flustered, she attempts to cover her embarrassment and tells him to "fill it up." After another such occasion she vows she will change stations if she must face "this up-frontery" each time she needs gas.

What are her alternatives?

For some people, direct feedback is the answer: "I'm too

old for that sweetheart line, so I'll tell you my name. It's Mrs. Mason. Perhaps you'll remember it since I come in often."

To Sadie this approach is also too up-front. "I want to be polite but impersonal because that is the way I would like him to treat me."

Here is Sadie's solution:

> First I needed to brace myself a bit. I did this each time just before driving into the station, saying to myself, "Sadie, get ready now. Deep breath. It's time to be neutral. Stay cool as the kids say. Relax." Then when he greeted me with that sweetheart stuff I tried very hard not to react at all but just calmly looked at him and said, "Young man, would you please fill the tank?"

> That was several months back. I followed through this way three times before he stopped calling me sweetheart. But as soon as he quit, I talked to him pleasantly. Now we're friendly. Maybe he still addresses other women that way but he and I have an unspoken understanding.

As soon as her gas station Casanova stopped his annoying greeting, Sadie responded quickly to reinforce the change. She also cued herself to relax and think. This special attention to our own behavior is important when using extinction, since neutral reactions are difficult to give. Finally, she modeled a more formal and polite verbal exchange which also cued the manager to the style she preferred.

Earlier we pointed out that extinction is most effective when used with certain other principles. This is especially true with the principle of rewarding an alternative action, to be discussed in the next chapter. You combine stopping one behavior with starting another that is preferred which you can then reward, as Sadie did. Of course, you would never use extinction simultaneously with satiation, because they are incompatible.

UNINTENTIONALLY EXTINGUISHING OTHERS' RESPONSES

In chance ways we contribute to the extinction of others' responses even when we do not wish to do so.

"Our son, Jamie, used to love to bake muffins," says Eileen, "but as he grew older we stopped encouraging him, really out of benign neglect and not sexism. Now I'm sorry. I wish he had learned more about cooking, but he's no longer interested."

Stephanie says, "There was a certain way that Seth made love to me that was so great, but I didn't ever tell him so. Why is it so hard to communicate?! Now he's changed."

"When I first became a division head," says Sigrid, "I made the error of not encouraging my people to work on ideas of their own. As a result, real innovations just didn't materialize." Sigrid's mistake was to extinguish creativity.

The three women just mentioned recognize how their *not* offering reinforcement contributed to others' giving up desirable behavior. We all need to be on the alert for this possibility.

Cautions About Using Extinction

DON'T USE WITH HARMFUL ACTIONS

Extinction should only be applied in situations where responses to be ended are not harmful to anyone. We would not intentionally want to overlook one child bullying another, just as we would not want to disregard child abuse or wife battering. Hurtfulness and violence cannot be ignored.

BE CONSISTENT

You are aware that all sources of reinforcement must be controlled if extinction is to work. This means that consistency in how we respond is essential.

Heidi and Kevin, both nineteen years old, belong to the same social group. Kevin begins to single Heidi out for special attention. Heidi is not interested and continually turns down his invitations to get together separately from the group. Kevin keeps trying. Now he has two tickets to a concert. When he asks Heidi and she hesitates, Kevin moves in. "C'mon, Heidi. It'll be terrific."

Heidi finally agrees to go with him and remarks to her girl friend, "But at least I made him wait a long time before I agreed to anything."

By giving in after continually saying no, Heidi reinforces Kevin's persistence beautifully. If she doesn't want his attention, she should say no and stick to it, or if necessary change her mind immediately so he is not reinforced for continuing to try. In no way can Heidi's responses be construed as quelling Kevin's interest.

DEAL WITH STRENGTHENED RESISTANCE

As you know, being ignored usually makes a person try harder before giving up. During this period, combating resistance by being consistently low-key or neutral is particularly difficult, as Heidi has shown with Kevin. It is hard not to give in, give up, or fight back. Knowing this in advance helps us be prepared.

OMIT BUT DON'T REMOVE REWARDS

Let's not mix up withholding rewards from people with taking away from them something that has already been given or promised. Although you might think the results are the same, they elicit quite different feelings.

If Heidi changes her mind and tells Kevin she doesn't want to go to the concert after all, she does not omit a reward (which would be the case if she did not accept in the first place); she removes one that has already been promised (by changing her mind). The effect on Kevin is hurtful. Taking away the promise does not ignore his interest, it punishes it. (More on this in Chapter twelve.)

AVOID CUTTING OFF COMMUNICATION

Extinction has the potential to damage or even end a relationship. Even though nonresponsiveness is an ideal way to stop certain kinds of actions, it easily interferes with spontaneous and positive communication that is vital to basic interaction between people; therefore it should be used sparingly and judiciously.

Time for Yourself #17

For a week take notice of the times you unintentionally give reinforcement to someone for actions you really do not like. Then keep a written record of similar situations and how you respond *neutrally*. Note the consequences.

Another Person's Action   Your Neutral Response   Consequences

CHAPTER ELEVEN

Alternative Actions: Rewarding Only Your Preferences

When Sam asked me to sew a button on his shirt
I said no, but that I'd be happy to show him how to
do it himself.

Cissy

I bit my lip to keep from speaking out,
but it was worth it.

Maggie

I didn't want to answer the question, so I
responded with a question of my own.

Mary Elizabeth

Now we come to the preferred way to stop habits we don't
want. You will recognize this method as the application of
two principles: reinforcement and extinction. When applying
this principle, not only is the first behavior eliminated but a
preferred one is developed in its place. Usually several alternative behaviors to the one to be stopped are available. The
new action may be opposite to the original (Cissy, above),

one that cannot take place simultaneously (Maggie), or one that is merely distracting (Mary Elizabeth).

Rewarding Incompatible
Alternatives
to Stop Your Own Actions

Self-defeating habits and anxieties common to many women can be turned around by rewarding selected alternatives to actions we wish to stop. **The Incompatible Alternative Principle: To stop any action, reward an alternative behavior that is inconsistent with or cannot be performed at the same time as the one you wish to end.** In each of the sections that follow, notice how an alternative response, once made specific and reinforced, interferes with an undesirable one in such a way that it creates the likelihood of a change in behavior.

REWARDING AN OPPOSITE BEHAVIOR

"I have this habit," says Cristina, "of questioning people when they offer to help me. Things like 'Do you honestly mean it?' 'But do you really have the time?' I even make up excuses to allow them to get out of their offer. I might say 'You're probably exhausted after working all day,' or 'I'm sure it's not a convenient hour for you.' I want to learn to respond to offers of assistance from people without questioning them, by simply answering 'How nice of you to ask. I'd like that.' or 'No, but thanks anyway.' "

Cristina's specific examples of the habit she wishes to stop and the opposite one she hopes to replace it with help her initiate the change she wants. Pleased with herself, she finds it takes less effort than she expects to stop questioning others when they offer to help her. She begins to take them at their word.

Marylou's problem is similar. Monitoring her own speech, she notices endings such as "Looks really dark outside, *doesn't it?*" "We need gas, *don't we?*" "It's a beautiful dress, *don't you think?*" *Marylou:* "This indecisiveness shows a lack of strength on my part. Now that I know I do this, I want to stop it. It affects how I come across to others."

Having clarified her starter goal, Marylou reinforces herself for nontentative comments. ("It looks dark outside." "We need gas." "It's a beautiful dress.") The old habits, well ingrained but no longer encouraged, disappear gradually. "I'm changing," says Marylou, "and I'm not going to ask if you agree."

Vanessa wants to stop blaming herself for problems that aren't her fault. "For example, the other day I was carrying a tray of food, and someone bumped into me because she clearly was not watching where she was going. The tray spilled and I found myself, as usual, saying, 'It's all my fault. I shouldn't have loaded my tray so full. Excuse me.' Well, it *wasn't* my fault, and I was furious with myself afterward."

Vanessa's recognition of this habit gives her a chance to develop a starter goal to stop it. For a while she may need to counter her self-imposed guilt with positive assurances that she is on the right track when she resists the temptation to assume responsibility for someone else's embarrassing moment. She may even arrange extrinsic rewards, but eventually feeling better because she no longer sabotages herself will be the real payoff.

Janette has just about stopped yelling at her children in the morning before school. ("You've lost your shoe *again?*" "Don't tell me you *still* haven't made your peanut butter sandwich!") Janette and her husband, Stan, also go to school each day, and they divide responsibilities for their kids. Talking it over, they decide that Janette needs Stan's support during the countdown before school takeoff but not as a fellow screamer. "Rather," says Janette, "on my days to get the kids ready, Stan is the audience for my *silences*. You might say he listens to me shutting up. Then, after the door closes and the kids run off to the bus, he gives me a big hug." With Stan's reinforcement Janette is becoming an ex-yeller in the mornings.

Rhonda offers an example of a personal habit she wants to change. "John asked me if I'd like to go to the beach with his friends on Saturday. I was so concerned about covering up the fact that I can't stand these friends of his that I gave totally unrealistic, *positive* feedback: 'Terrific! I can hardly wait!' You'd think I'd been trying to set it up for weeks. Talk about self-betrayal! I want to stop being overwhelmingly positive to cover up my negative feelings."

Changing this well-established pattern does not happen quickly, probably because the incidents occur infrequently. But Rhonda is determined. She keeps herself alert to occasions that are likely to throw her and develops a repertory of ambiguous stop-gap responses to use to delay her answers until she is ready with an honest yes or no. ("I'll sure think about it." "That's a real possibility." "I'll let you know when I get myself organized.") Then she makes certain she reinforces her efforts. In this way she gradually replaces her misleading answers with ones that are more reasonable and more truthful.

REWARDING A BEHAVIOR
THAT CANNOT BE PERFORMED
AT THE SAME TIME AS ANOTHER

Mimi's problem is gaining weight. She suspects the cause is related to an evening cocktail hour that has gotten out of hand—caloric niblets with a caloric drink before dinner. Mimi loves to swim and decides to capitalize on it. "I have rear-ranged my day to schedule swimming before supper. The public pool is close to home. With swimming I feel invigorated, get the exercise I need, and cut down on my caloric intake as well. There isn't time to swim before dinner and have cocktails (with junk food), too." As long as Mimi considers swimming a rewarding trade-off, she has an excellent chance of success.

Bea is embarrassed by her habit of compulsively knocking her knees together when she sits in a tense situation ("such as taking tests, trying to get a word in edgewise with others, or attempting to cover my annoyance at someone else's comments"). Searching for an incompatible response to help herself stop the habit, Bea brags about her simple solution— merely crossing her legs whenever these occasions occur. Such physically incompatible actions are also known to help control facial tics and other nervous mannerisms. They also work in situations such as the one described in a recent TV soap opera:

To reduce Ashley's dilemma to basics, she can't decide whether she loves Dennis or Chuck. Finally she realizes that Chuck is the one for her. With lingering fondness (and D-minor music in the background), she faces the unpleasant task of informing Dennis. Later she tells a friend, "I had to sit on my hands to keep from hugging him as I have so often in the past. He had to realize I meant it this time. No tender goodbyes." Instead of her former action (hugging), Ashley substitutes another that can't be performed at the same time (hand sitting). Even soap operas use the Incompatible Alternative Principle.

We already know from Chapter five that practicing relaxation techniques while anxious gradually reduces stress as we gain the comfortable feelings associated with relaxation. It is another way of stopping one behavior by developing another that cannot be performed at the same time.

REWARDING A DISTRACTING BEHAVIOR

The simplest way to reward an alternative is to distract ourselves. After her husband's death, Claudia finds that immersing herself in her office work relieves the pain from her loss by not giving her time to dwell on it most of the day. Hallie, uncomfortable in closed elevators when she is by herself, sings a song out loud when she must face riding alone. Recently, going to sleep at night is difficult for Scotty. Attributing this to thinking about problems that arise during the day in her new job, she now distracts herself from thinking about them before bedtime by watching TV until she is sleepy.

Notice that these women find pleasant reinforcing distractors. Otherwise their original behavior is likely to be more desirable than the distracting alternatives. Even with planned reinforcement, when you consider a starter goal using this principle, evaluate whether the new behavior holds sufficient value for you. If not, consider another so you'll be more likely to succeed.

Rewarding Incompatible Alternatives to Stop Others' Actions

To prevent others from imposing themselves on us either unintentionally or deliberately, we can reward them for the same kinds of incompatible alternative actions we use to stop ourselves.

"The men in my family," says Dale, "expect me to wash *their* dishes, clean up *their* messes, and take care of *their* children, namely my nieces. I don't like being expected to perform certain tasks just because I'm female. They are real chauvinists. If I am subtle dealing with the problem I won't be heard." But Dale also feels that a strong display of her feelings is equally self-defeating. "Then they tease me." To hold her own in what she considers a reasonable way, she turns down their outright requests in a firm but low-key manner. However, she makes clear she will *help* them with the jobs or even at times perform them alone *provided* they offer to do something in exchange. Their reward is her assistance, but it is offered only when they share some responsibility, a change from their former actions. To be effective, Dale's method for coping with the men in her family should be consistent.

"My father has the habit of asking me personal questions about my love life," says Kathy, now in her late twenties. "This is despite my telling him I don't want to talk about it. So now I ignore him as much as I can until he moves along to another topic, but then I give my complete attention."

Kathy claims she and her father have a good relationship but this curiosity about her personal life annoys her. "Trying to change him has not been a complete success," Kathy says later, "but it sure beats having arguments." One possibility for her lack of success may be that Kathy's father obtains just enough information from her to *reinforce* his question-asking rather than to stop it.

Jena responds "blandly, to say the least" when Dick phones her early in the morning but reacts enthusiastically when he calls later in the day. "I don't like being awakened by a ringing phone, even from Dick." Some people would prefer to speak frankly to a caller who wakes them up, but Jena, at least with Dick, wants to be less direct and still make her point, so she carefully reinforces only those times she prefers him to phone.

At the office party Mary Jo finds herself paired off with Travis, a womanizing sales representative. His comments are suggestive, and she realizes his hand, having touched her shoulder, is moving almost imperceptibly down her back. Unable to move easily from her corner, she nevertheless turns her body around to face him directly, dislodging his hand and saying, "You mentioned you were in Kansas City. Did you spend time at the Crown Center?"

Mary Jo's diversionary tactics stop Travis's previous action and introduce a new subject. However, she carefully does not communicate to him any special interest in his trip, aware that she might then reinforce his previous behavior. Shortly thereafter she extricates herself and moves along.

Most women have dealt with situations similar to Mary Jo's. If you have, and if you handled it the same way, you have already used a simple version of the Incompatible Alternative Principle. For yourself, or with others, this principle is one of the best.

CHAPTER TWELVE

Relief from Unpleasantness: Its Own Reward

That remark was like a slap in the face. How can
I be kind when she treats me this way?

Melissa

Whew! I'm glad that's over.

Tracy

This is a book about caring. Nevertheless it would be incomplete without an understanding of the use and effect of punishment. We all need to understand the many ways punishment intrudes on our everyday lives so we can control it better. Some people subscribe to the idea that the best way to stop a behavior is to punish it. Not so. For this reason this principle about stopping undesirable habits emphasizes the *ending* of punishment rather than the punishment itself. But before we look at it we need to be clear about what punishment includes and how it affects people.

What Punishment Includes

Anything unpleasant or painful is punishing—whether physical or emotional, especially when we see no way to terminate it.

PHYSICAL PUNISHMENT

Dealing with physical violence is beyond the scope of this book. People with these problems need the help of on-the-turf professionals—a local physician, clergyman, or the appropriate community agency. Less flagrant examples of physical hurtfulness do warrant our attention. Occasional spanking, slapping, kicking, pinching, arm-twisting, and hair-pulling are also punishing.

Although we think of physical punishment as meted out by one person to another, it is also self-imposed, often through overindulgence. ("After that big meal I forced myself to throw up." "So I smoke too much. So I'll die of cancer." "I gardened when my knee was still sore and now it's really killing me.") Sometimes we deny the fact that we physically abuse ourselves.

EMOTIONAL PUNISHMENT

All of us are both givers and receivers of emotional punishment, and much of the time we don't realize it. As women we especially need to be on the look-out for ways we unintentionally punish ourselves because of our earlier social conditioning—for example, by emphasizing our failures instead of our improvements, by maintaining fears that limit our growth, or by exposing ourselves unduly to the brunt of others' criticism.

When you feel unhappy, ask yourself, "How am I contributing to my own misery?" Answers to this private question are not easy to come by, but probing may give you clues to starter goals that will eliminate self-punishing habits related to your unhappiness. Search for solutions rather than ways to legitimize your problems. Blaming the way you are on what happened in your past does not help you grow.

We also suffer abuse as victims of "double binds."

DELLA: With little kids to take care of I see my choices as being a concerned parent and ignoring my writing career or writing and ignoring my kids. I tried doing both and the distractions gave me writer's block. So right now I'm opting for saving my sanity but losing my mind.

176

EDITH: When I exert control in my own business I risk turning both women and men off because I'm being "masculine."

GWEN: I'm frustrated when my husband won't share the workload at home and my children see us modeling a marriage style that is inequitable. Yet if I make an issue of it we end up arguing in front of them. I don't like to model fighting either.

Frustration from situations that pull us in divergent directions is punishing. By definition, double binds hold no pat solutions. To resolve them we either must set our goal to take a given path despite odds or set our goal to accept the conflict and live with it. But much personal punishment can occur before we work out these damned-if-we-dos and damned-if-we-don'ts in our lives.

People take all kinds of emotional abuse from others. We punish each other by nagging, manipulating, offering unsolicited advice, remaining passive, teasing, being sarcastic, being too dependent, acting insulting ("You're a fool if you do that." "I can't believe you actually said that."), or name-calling ("stupid," "wimp," "brittle brain," "male chauvinist").

Remember that broken promises are punishing. Were you ever offered a toy as a child and then denied it because you misbehaved? As an adult did you ever plan to attend an event that was cancelled at the last moment? When you recall the feeling of unfair treatment or disappointment because something was taken away that you thought you could count on, you will understand why broken promises are also considered punishment.

In an intensified way, the same anguish occurs between adults in a close relationship when one partner takes away (or suddenly stops doing) something desirable that has come to be depended upon and assumed by the other, even though no specific agreement was ever made. It is like an unwritten contract. If the second person views the change as a promise (inferred from past behavior) that has now been broken, the result is a disequilibrium in the partnership that must be resolved.

Deborah is a housewife, 37 years old. She and Todd have been married fifteen years and have three children—eight, twelve, and fourteen. While Deborah stayed home to care for

"Why can't you ever think of a socko exit line?"

WE MAY PUNISH OTHERS WHEN THEY FAIL OUR EXPECTATIONS

the children, Todd was out climbing the corporate ladder. His work now includes coast-to-coast conferencing and heavy administrative responsibilities. During the first fourteen years of their marriage Todd spent time on weekends taking care of household repair jobs—rescreening doors, touching up scratched walls, reglueing floor tiles, cleaning the gutters. Deborah often helped. But now Todd, burdened with heavier responsibilities, no longer wants to be a household handyman and proclaims, "I've reached a point in life where my time is worth more than my money. Deborah, please get somebody in here to do these jobs. I want my weekends free."

Deborah's reaction is one of dismay and hurt. She suddenly sees Todd as losing interest in their home and no longer keen to share time with her. An unspoken promise, inferred from his past behavior, has been broken.

Deborah might have felt differently if Todd had thought of his family chores in terms of an unspoken agreement in their marriage when he brought up the subject of a change. Then he might have included her as he would any business associate in a decision-making process involving two people: "You know, Deb, we could really pay someone to do these chores now. It would let us have more time for other things on weekends. I'd really like that after working under pressure all week. How about you? What do you think?"

Cueing in this manner is more apt to produce an outcome amenable to both partners.

The women's movement creates many situations similar to Deborah's and Todd's, where women, because of their socialization, make unspoken promises to their partners or children that they later question and want to change. If we as women recognize that our changes, however justified, may be viewed by others who are affected by them as promises we are breaking, we may look with a different perspective at ways we go about initiating our changes. We may then carefully cue others to our feelings and involve them in our planning, consistently showing appreciation for even partial efforts on their parts to accommodate us. This is what Sara Benson did earlier with her husband, Richard. Combinations of better timing, advance cueing, and reinforcement of others' efforts all make the changes we deserve seem less punitive and more palatable to others. They are not foolproof, since resistance is based on many factors, but they can make real differences.

How Punishment Affects People

People respond to punishing experiences in ways that underscore the dangerous side effects:

1. Punishment creates resistance and avoidance. People feeling punished are likely to fight back (with accompanying tensions, arguments, or even violence), withdraw (think of the husband who hides behind his newspaper or the housewife who is a closet alcoholic), or actively escape (obtain a divorce, become a workaholic, find another partner on the side).

2. Punishment corrodes a close relationship. Just as honest positive feedback spirals a relationship upward, punishing interactions within a relationship spiral it downward. ("That remark was like a slap in the face." "How can I be kind when she treats me this way?" "I never know how to take him. His teasing makes me so uncomfortable.")

3. Punishment fosters neurotic behavior. If the punishment is sufficiently severe, people who see no escape from it over an extended period of time suffer from anxiety, irrational fears, and depression. They feel boxed in with no way of getting out.

4. Punishers are often rewarded—at first. The initial feeling of release one has from getting even or getting tough when annoyed is reinforcing. However, it is usually followed by guilt about the punishment that has been inflicted. Claudette despairs because she is physically unable to bear children, but people ask her why she is waiting so long to have a family. "Tell me," she says, "how I can get back at them when they ask such a hurtful question." Claudette would experience great initial joy at punishing her "tormentors" but her problem would remain and guilt would undoubtedly compound it. When people want to get even with others, the best way to protect their own feelings in the long run is to focus on how they might change their own thinking instead. Claudette might learn through simple rehearsal to give the true explanation: "Unfortunately, I can't have children." Or she might learn to restructure her own view: "Wouldn't those people feel terrible if they knew all the facts."

5. Victims may also feel rewarded. Some people enjoy being punished because it gives them attention or alleviates their own guilt. The punishment hurts but becomes the price paid for the reward received.

Others just don't suffer. A women's support group invited men to its meeting. When the men refused to take the agenda seriously and didn't "settle down" to participate, the women declared that unless they did they wouldn't be invited to any further meetings. Too late did they realize that was just what the men hoped for. The "punishment" was actually a reward.

The use of punishment harbors many drawbacks, and these are the reasons it is considered a last-resort measure. However, when you do find it necessary there is a special—and limited—use known as negative reinforcement which is less dangerous.

A Safer Alternative
to All-Out Punishment

The Negative Reinforcement Principle: To stop a certain action, end a mildly punishing situation immediately when the behavior improves. As Tracy so aptly states at the beginning of the chapter, this is the "Whew! I'm glad that's over" principle. Its effectiveness is based on the correct timing for *ending* the punishment: Punitive measures prevail only as long as the response is unacceptable. *Relief from the unpleasantness constitutes the reinforcement for stopping.* Later the new behavior may also be rewarded in the customary ways.

APPLYING NEGATIVE REINFORCEMENT
TO STOP YOUR OWN ACTIONS

The timer on Mollie's electric stove in her studio apartment buzzes with a piercing noise until it is turned off. Mollie's daily routine is to walk home for lunch at noon, then lie down on her sofa to read the morning paper until time to return to work. She uses the buzzer as negative reinforcement to get her back on her feet. It is not just a cue, it is a mildly punishing (irritating) noise that ends only after Mollie stops reading, gets up, and turns it off.

Rorey, recently divorced, faces tasks that were formerly assumed by her husband. All too often she finds herself handling them by asking men to assist her rather than figuring out how to do them herself. She obtains help from a close woman friend in order to change. "We talk on the phone every day, and I've asked her to chew me out if she catches me leaning on men, especially other women's husbands. So far she's caught me asking a neighbor to change a ceiling lightbulb and to unclog the sink disposal." Rorey's help from another person to "bug" her raises several questions. Have other principles with fewer negative side-effects been tried first? Might not Rorey become an increasingly dishonest reporter of her own actions? Could this method damage her relationship with her friend? Is Rorey's self-esteem on the line? Why not spotlight her improved performances rather than her errors? (Then Rorey would have a better chance to feel good about herself.)

Negative reinforcement can be built into situations. Rose points this out when she wears clothes too tight for herself after gaining weight. "I wear them unaltered. Then I'm uncomfortable until I slim down. It's a relief to get back to my normal weight."

Notice that in the examples above, women have already figured out exactly what responses they want to stop, the aversiveness itself is mild, and each one (including Rorey) is in charge of terminating it. When we use negative reinforcement on ourselves, there should be no question about who controls the aversiveness. We should.

APPLYING NEGATIVE REINFORCEMENT TO STOP OTHERS' ACTIONS

Leigh's long-distance calls to her boyfriend are going sour. Art continually interrupts and interjects questions about her activities into their conversations: "Why did you do that?" "What made you bring that up?" "How come that's so important?"

Over time, Leigh tries unsuccessfully to change the subject (to reward an alternative). She also tries extinction ("Okay, Art, whatever . . . "), and satiation ("Pardon? . . . Pardon? . . . Pardon? . . . "). Extinction and satiation, you will recall, are never used successfully together, and Leigh realized this too late.

At last she turns to negative reinforcement. "Art, this is ridiculous. I think we should get off the phone." No results.

Then finally, "When you feel like talking to me without turning it into one of these question sessions, call me. Don't count on my calling you next time. I'll just wait till you want to talk reasonably." Art says he doesn't want to hang up, but Leigh tells him she is going to and she does.

Art called her the next day and was extremely friendly. Leigh reported that he didn't directly apologize, but he did say he was upset with himself. "It was a good conversation, and the following two were good, too. I think we are getting back to the way we were before all this started."

Let's not oversimplify by assuming that Leigh's and Art's relationship will remain improved indefinitely. Nevertheless, Leigh has made her own limitations known, and this cannot help but clarify their communication. Leigh gives a warning first, then follows through rather than continuing with idle threats. Art is free to end the punishing effect of her hanging up as soon as he ends the heckling. When he does, there are pleasurable results rather than recriminations. These are conditions that help make negative reinforcement effective with others.

Confrontation is punishing. If it ends when behavior improves it is negative reinforcement. One day Marcia, dressed appropriately for her particular government job, wears a T-shirt on the front of which is printed two popular candy bars. Noticing the shirt, a man in her office approaches her. *Marcia:* "He leers and giggles as he looks at my chest and says 'Which one?' I ask him to repeat what he said, and he does. So later I placed a note on his desk saying I didn't think what he said was funny, and how would he like it if someone talked that way to his wife or daughter? The note worked. He appeared stunned and ashamed, and apologized."

Marcia mentioned, however, that her male co-worker was not comfortable around her the rest of the time she remained in that department. Sometimes such direct confrontation is the only way, but since it can affect the future of a relationship, the following example illustrates a less punishing approach that lessens this possibility, still using negative reinforcement.

Kim at age 36 works in a middle-management position. Interaction with her immediate superior, Larry, has been satisfactory in the past, but now Kim is seething. She just left a meeting in which she clearly heard Larry say to several other men, "I'll have my girl take care of these requisitions." That "girl" had to be Kim. Her anger is so intense that her impulse is to confront him immediately. The question is whether she is capable of stopping to think first. With effort she does. "Just for now I'll give Larry the benefit of blatant ignorance over blatant insensitivity."

Then Kim waits for the first opportunity when Larry is alone and they are not working under a pressured deadline. With her *SUDS* level considerably lower now and having rehearsed what she wants to say, she approaches and talks to him privately: "Larry, I'm sure you wouldn't do it intentionally, but it demeans me to be referred to as 'your girl' in the office." This launches them into a dispassionate discussion that Larry is nevertheless not likely to forget. But he does not suffer the added humiliation of being confronted angrily in front of others. Discomfort from talking with Kim is the only aversiveness he suffers *provided* he changes how he refers to her. If he does not she still has the option of stronger protest, but right now their relationship remains intact, an asset for Kim as well as for Larry.

The Bradshaws are a traditional family. Their dinner hour is 6:30. If Brad is detained at the office, he has agreed to call Diane to let her know. Then she will decide whether to wait or go ahead and feed the children, and she will have Brad's meal ready when he arrives later. After several occasions when Brad arrives home late but forgets to phone her, Diane suggests a change in policy. "Let's agree that dinner is firm if you don't call and that the children and I will begin eating at six thirty. They get hungry waiting. If you don't phone and are late, you warm up your own dinner when you get here. Whenever you arrive on time or phone so I know how late you'll be, I'll have your meal ready for you."

The new agreement gives Brad more responsibility for his own actions and it takes the problem of hungry children off Diane's shoulders. If Brad is unhappy warming up his own dinner, he knows that if he arrives home on time or phones it will not be necessary. He can terminate this "unpleasantness" himself. Previously, Diane really rewarded his forgetfulness by accommodating him whenever he showed up.

Ted and Josie have lived together for four years. They divide household chores, and Ted is responsible for plumbing repairs. Right now a toilet runs continually, and in her quest to activate Ted, Josie proclaims to a friend, "I'm not going to touch a thing. But when Ted finally does get around to fixing it, I'm going to give him hell."

Certainly this is not negative reinforcement. Negative reinforcement is based on a sense of relief as a result of a behavior change. Giving Ted hell after he completes the job is simply punishing him for doing the repair work. If her idea is to cue him, she must do so in advance, never after the fact. If Josie shows appreciation after the job is complete, Ted is more likely to come through the next time.

No *Time for Yourself* project is suggested for the Negative Reinforcement Principle. Due to its harmful side-effects we do not encourage its use. Perhaps the most meaningful project would be one suggesting that each time you think about changing a behavior by punishing it, deliberately ask yourself what other principles might work first.

CHAPTER THIRTEEN

Self-Sabotage Messages: Encountering and Countering

A little kingdom I possess,
Where thoughts and feelings dwell;
And very hard the task I find
Of governing it well.
Louisa May Alcott

We are all apt to believe what the world believes about us.
George Eliot (Mary Ann Evans)

Maribel tells of a terrifying recurring dream she had as a child: "It was of a wolf-tiger animal always about to spring on me. The image came from a trim strip at the top of the wallpaper in my bedroom. The dream slowly went away as I forced myself to picture me riding astride this creature every time it appeared."

Maribel gained control over the haunting image high on her wall by changing the message she gave herself about it. While what elicits the messages we receive in our lives may be unchangeable, how we *process* the content involves personal choices that can make real differences to us. The creature didn't change for Maribel, but how she thought about it did.

In this chapter we look at ways to process the content of our thoughts.

Ways Women Sabotage
Themselves

If the messages we give ourselves are self-defeating, maybe even distorting reality, we become our own undercover adversaries. We create irrational self-thoughts. Many of these messages are based upon private assumptions we don't realize we hold. The following categories represent thought processes that sabotage our own efforts.

GIVING FAULTY SELF-INSTRUCTIONS

We have seen how negative self-prophecies cue us to fail. Faulty self-instructions are similar and produce similar results.

Sharon and Audrey are both in their late twenties and work in Washington, D.C., where they share a house with several others. While Audrey is outgoing and likes to direct people, Sharon is quiet and compliant. Gradually, however, Sharon begins to feel used. One morning when Audrey says she needs to exchange cooking times with her and wants to borrow her car that night, Sharon complains bitterly to another housemate, "Look what Audrey is making me do."

From this remark we know that Sharon will (reluctantly) tell herself to follow through with Audrey's wishes. Since she mistakenly assumes she has no other choices, she does not consider several alternative ways to instruct herself such as: "Look what I am letting Audrey do to me." "It's up to Audrey to find a willing housemate to exchange her cooking turn with. Tell her to look for someone else." "It's your car. You are in charge, not Audrey. If you don't want her to use it, say so." or "Help her out because you really want to but not because she makes you do it." Instead, Sharon unintentionally distorts reality and will give a self-defeating answer. She will exchange cooking times and loan her car.

Millie thinks about why she chatters nonstop when a conversation lags, especially with male friends. "I'm a marshmallow given to guilt if I'm not carrying the burden of entertaining." Under the assumption that it is up to her not to let lapses of conversation occur, Millie gives herself instructions to fill in the silences at any cost. She doesn't consider alternative self-instructions, such as "Millie, if you wait before you plunge in, maybe others will have something to say." or "Millie, relax. Silence is far more agreeable than listening to someone's compulsive talking." Instead, Millie sabotages herself by following self-instructions that are socially detrimental to her. She jumps in, takes over, and chatters nonstop.

At work Ginger is asked to move into another department in which accounting skills are an important aspect of the job. While it means an advancement for her, she decides not to consider it because her accounting background is limited. Ginger gives herself the instructions, "Since I don't have all the skills, I'm not going to try." She doesn't think of telling herself "I can learn new skills I don't have" or "I'll explain that I'll expect help for awhile but would like the advancement." Ginger does not allow herself even a small risk in order to move ahead.

Then there is Marilyn. She proudly signs up for an auto mechanics class. "Nobody's going to tell me I'm a person who doesn't know how things work in my own car." Armed with paper and pencil, Marilyn sets out for her first class. On her pad she prepares a left-hand column next to her note-taking labeled "Self-Statements." Under this she jots down those secretly expressed feelings, those inner voices, that come to her during the three-hour class period. Here are excerpts from that column, all of them recorded during the first session.

"Where are the women? Dear God. Let's have some women here. You're going to be the only one, Marilyn."

"Come on, M. Give 'em your fake smile of confidence."

"I bet everyone in this room has changed a tire except me."

"I can tell I'm not going to fit in with these people."

"I'll ask some guy to help me. What am I thinking?! I'm too dependent on men."

"Dumb-dumb. You're just not mechanical."

"Transmission? Shit. How do I know what that is? He doesn't even say. I'm behind already."

"That's a terrible question. You'll be laughed at. Don't ask."

"Right back in the old mold. The I'm-just-a-woman routine. Marilyn, how could you?"

"I hate this. Just hate it. Why am I here? I'm simply not right for this. Why did I ever think I needed it?"

"I don't want to learn this junk."

"Boring."

Most people, of course, don't go around writing down their inner thoughts while at the same time taking class notes. Marilyn does so to obtain personal insights, and the evidence turns out to be pertinent to her self-understanding. With negative self-instruction cueing, she sabotages her own efforts to learn about car maintenance, programming herself for actions opposite to those she claims to want. Is it likely, for instance, that she will be open to learning about transmissions when she has just told herself she is dumb and not mechanical? That she will be comfortable in the group when she tells herself she doesn't fit in? That she will listen carefully when she declares herself bored?

Sharon, Millie, Ginger, and Marilyn are not the only ones. Are any of these potentially faulty self-instructions other women have made a part of your own repertory?

"Don't go alone. People might suspect you don't have friends."

"Don't speak up. It might prove embarrassing."

"If I don't flirt a lot, men won't pay attention to me."

"My family always comes first. Of course I'll put my own needs aside."

"It's too risky."

"I don't understand what goes on in that lab so there is no point in my doing the reading assignment for it."

"It's not up to me. There are guys around to take over."

"I'll play dumb. Then I won't have to get involved."

Thus we give ourselves instructions about what our limitations "should be" and further internalize the notion that we are only so-so, thereby cueing ourselves to respond in so-so ways. Pay attention to your self-instructions so you don't set off a self-defeating chain of events.

LABELING SITUATIONS OR PERSONS

Previously we discussed how deliberate labeling helps us distinguish between what we do or do not want to model. Now we'll see how labeling *unintentionally* can lead us to self-sabotage.

Think for a moment of a ballet in which a woman and a man perform a *pas de deux* but their conventional roles are reversed. The woman assists the man in his pirouette and after he spins he gracefully falls into her arms. Finally she lifts him dramatically high above her head and carries him away. This scene is unsettling to think about because we have already labeled the opposite roles as masculine and feminine.

In everyday life we may unwittingly stick similar imaginary labels, like name tags, on events or persons (including ourselves) and then expect everyone to act accordingly. See if you agree with these:

> "It's my husband's responsibility (to reconcile our account each month, carve the turkey, make the major family decisions)."
>
> "Married women don't go on vacations without their husbands."
>
> "Before marriage a woman should have more male than female friends."
>
> "After marriage a woman should have more female than male friends."
>
> "If I'm not invited it proves they don't like me."
>
> "I'll be considered snobby if I turn people down, even if I'm busy."
>
> "Men can't be trusted."
>
> "Women are lousy bosses."
>
> "If others don't live up to my expectations, there must be something wrong with them."

Intentionally ending situations for which we receive few or no rewards may mistakenly be labeled selfishness. Tina decides she doesn't want to meet friends from her old job who plan a lunch reunion. Previous get-togethers have not been re-

190

warding to her because the conversations usually center on past events and current child-care problems. Tina has no children. She does not care to impose topics of her own choosing on the group so she stops attending. "I know it's selfish, but there's nothing in it for me."

While Tina knows she wants to separate from a group with which she has little or nothing left in common, she still burdens herself with a "selfish" label that easily promotes personal guilt. Yet she unselfishly declines to impose her own interests on others. She might better say to herself, "These people do not need me. We are growing in different directions. It is good that I realize I can move away."

Learning to notice the labels we are already using is as important as knowing when to label.

EXAGGERATING THE IMPORTANCE OF THINGS

Labeling from hidden assumptions also occurs when we misjudge the significance of things, often making them seem more important than they really are:

"If he really cared he would understand how I felt."

"If I can't do something well I don't want to do it at all."

"I should be liked by everybody."

"I shouldn't spend time on things that aren't worthwhile."

"Company meals should be elaborate so guests know I care enough."

"I would just die if my children didn't behave well in public."

"It's essential for women to look and act feminine."

Absolutist thinking is a result of labeling. Without realizing it, we stop allowing ourselves latitude about how we look at situations. The world appears black or white. Having only one "right" answer, we sabotage ourselves by ignoring other possible choices from the shades in between.

NOT TAKING CHARGE OF PERSONAL FEELINGS

Anger, guilt, frustration, depression—these feelings are well known to us. While they may well be legitimate, how we deal with them can be self-destructive. Contrast Sybil and Carrie, both in their sixties and widows for over a year.

Sybil cannot talk directly about Hugh's death but does nonetheless give ample evidence of her state of mind. Comments such as "I just don't feel up to having people over yet," and "I've had to let the garden go this year. I've simply no interest in it," set the tone of her conversations. Most circumstances in her life she chooses to interpret negatively or with little enthusiasm. Life for Sybil is depressingly tough.

Carrie also grieves. Many places and incidents remind her of life with her husband and continue to trigger memories that consume her at times when she senses she might be giving attention to other things. It is so easy to let her mind wander that she feels she has overindulged herself, and she now wants to stop. Carrie decides to allow herself to think briefly about her memories as they occur, but not to dwell on them because doing so holds built-in rewards for living in the past. "Working on this," she says, "is what Paul would want me to do. I still grieve, of course, but life goes on. I've got to place this sorrow in a larger perspective and allow other parts of my life to catch up."

Both of these women understand the need to release their grief rather than to bottle it up. Now, however, the two women view their similar situations quite differently. Carrie begins cueing herself to change with positive self-instructions. Sybil continues to view herself in mourning, thereby maintaining (and encouraging) her low spirits. It is as if she instructs herself: "There is nothing I can do. I can't stop feeling this way."

Judith faces another crisis. Her divorce from Bert has been final for two months. "Right now I feel completely out of step. I'm terribly isolated socially. I feel guilty about putting the children through all this, plus I don't have skills to do anything on my own."

One of the steps Judith can take to make her life more livable is to choose an alternative way to view her situation. She might say to herself, "Right now I'm in the process of solving a crisis in my life that a lot of other women also face. I know how painful it is, but at least it's not my unique problem. Others have survived it and adjusted well. I can, too. I've got to think of the steps I can take on my own. Then I will begin to gain more of a sense of control." Judith has the choice of treating her situation as the challenge of a large single event in her life or as a permanent state over which she has little or no control.

Maureen is the highest-level woman executive in a large company. She handles affirmative action issues, especially regarding women, often listening to complaints from subordinates and talking over problems with their superiors to negotiate changes. "It's pressure, pressure, pressure all day every day."

Although she receives high praise for job performance, Maureen confides that she is "terribly unhappy. You probably won't believe this, but I frequently go home at night and throw pans on my kitchen floor to cope with my frustration." Maureen's work record camouflages her personal needs. She absorbs friction, recognizes injustices, and knows too well the meaning of the phrase, "It's lonely at the top," because her male counterparts do not understand many of the issues. But although Maureen takes charge with others' feelings, she does not deal sufficiently with her own.

Sometimes we construct unrealistic images of ourselves that then sabotage us when we neglect our personal needs. For example, no one can indefinitely absorb anger and pressure without a release. Throwing pans is an outlet, but Maureen needs to find other, better ways to relieve her own pressures— actively searching for other top executive women to talk to, arranging a personal exercise program, and insisting on spaces of time to do whatever she pleases are possible starters. However, she does not do any of these things. She eventually resigns her position and lives off her earnings for ten months before she enters another job with less money and less responsibility. Maureen becomes a victim of job burnout and personal exhaustion.

Although extenuating circumstances can immobilize us and make it difficult to take control of our feelings, sometimes we assume we cannot change what is happening when in fact we can.

Changing the Messages

The Countering Principle: To stop self-sabotaging actions, focus on specific ways you give yourself irrational messages and change those messages to ones of self-support. As our awareness of how we sabotage ourselves increases we look for ways to counter our own actions. Glenna testifies: "I start by waging a little war in my mind." Rica puts it more bluntly: "I give myself a mental kick in the butt." Give Glenna and Rica credit for their courage in admitting they need to change their messages; however, their solutions lack operational credibility. Let's examine more reliable ways to change self-sabotaging messages to ones of self-support.

FOCUSING ATTENTION ON SELF–THOUGHTS

Occasionally it's so easy to recognize our own irrational thoughts that we think we notice all of them, but then *that* is an irrational thought. Self-sabotaging most often results from ideas we don't realize we have, so focusing our full attention on our thought processes is important. Here are two tips that will help:

Deliberately verbalize what you tell yourself. Bringing these thoughts to the surface will help you know what they really are. They won't be as fuzzy. There are several ways to do this. You can express them by talking out loud to yourself, listening carefully so that you can then clarify. You can write them out on paper. After doing this, put your writing aside and return later for a fresh look to clarify and analyze. Or you can "air" these inner ideas with a friend who is a good listener. Her or his feedback can help, but you are the ultimate clarifier about what your real thoughts are.

Probe for hidden assumptions. As your underlying thoughts become clearer, review the ways in which people sabotage themselves. Ask: "Am I, without realizing it, giving myself faulty instructions? Am I labeling the event or the person I'm thinking about unrealistically? Am I exaggerating the importance of the situation? Am I taking charge of my feelings or letting my feelings take charge of me?" Once we focus on what needs changing, there are several ways to go about it.

COUNTERING IRRATIONAL THOUGHTS

Countering is simply a way of talking back to ourselves purposefully. The more accurately we perceive our irrational thoughts, the better we can devise effective counterstatements to refute them.

Sheila, for instance, feels so inadequate in her new sales job that she wants to quit. There are too many rules about how to run a computerized register. Her self-message is "You are not as smart as the others who work here." When she looks for counters to this message, she selects one true statement that she can use as a counter that fits her situation. She repeats it to herself whenever she worries about the register: "No one here has learned to figure out complicated car rental rates like I did on my last job." This countering statement helps Sheila survive insecurities from an unfamiliar situation.

Similarly, Fran counters feelings of helplessness by reciting to herself times when she does have some power: "My children depend on me." "My health has improved because I made myself stay on my diet." "My mother relies on my judgment about what clothes look best on her." She repeats such counters whenever she needs them. Doing so is one way for Fran to combat feelings of helplessness. (Of course she

195

needs to work on starter goals to make her feel better about herself, too.)

The purpose of countering is to help end old irrational thoughts by refuting them with statements we believe to be true. The following counters apply to many situations:

"I did the best I could."
"Worry is nonproductive."
"The world won't come to an end."
"Bullshit. That's not logical. Stop and think."
"Steady, babe. This won't last forever."

On the other hand, these counters are more situation-specific:

THOUGHT: People laugh at me.
COUNTER: Others may prize my individuality as I do.
THOUGHT: I'm just a mediocre person.
COUNTER: I'm the only me in the whole world.
THOUGHT: I really stick out in a crowd.
COUNTER: It's okay to be an original occasionally.
THOUGHT: I'm never lucky at anything.
COUNTER: I'm not going to reward myself with self-pity.
THOUGHT: Nothing's going right in my world.
COUNTER: I've got my health, a steadfast friend, and money for groceries. I'm well off in comparison to many.

Several counters for a given irrational self-thought are usually better than just one, but of the several you arrive at, one or two will strike you as more effective than the others. These can be used a number of times to help refute a particular irrational idea.

Here are some ways to strengthen countering. Mona wants to end her irrational self-thought, namely: "Tom's parents aren't going to like me." Her first move: As soon as she realizes she has this notion, she immediately employs thought-stopping by saying sharply to herself, *"Stop!"* Then she quickly follows that command with all the countering statements she can think of. Her second move: She writes down her counters. This enables her to refer and add to them later. It fixes them in her mind. Then after she has written down several, her third move: She rank-orders each counter according to its effectiveness. Thus the counters to her concern that Tom's parents won't like her and her rank-ordering are as follows:

Counter	Rank
How can I say that! They haven't even met me.	4
Tom says they really appreciated my note.	5
After Lil, they may even be relieved.	3
Other people usually like me.	6
Tom's little dog likes me.	7
Tom has told me he likes me a lot.	2
I'm good at making positive impressions on boyfriends' families.	1

Time for Yourself #20

Each day for three days think of one familiar irrational self-thought and write it down. Then record as many counters as you can think of. At the end of each day, rank-order all counters on the basis of their effectiveness.

Day	Irrational Self-Thought	Counters	Rank

TURNING SELF-INSTRUCTIONS AROUND

We can find other vantage points from which to view some messages. ("Me Jane, you Tarzan.") This holds true for many negative self-instructions. Say to yourself:

"My hunger pangs are a cue to my becoming thinner" rather than hungrier.

"My boyfriend's stilted way of expressing his feelings means he's trying" rather than that he doesn't care.

"Expect things to go right" when you tend to look for trouble.

"Expect things to go wrong" when you're too much of a perfectionist.

"It's okay to be anxious" when confronting change.

"This shows I have the courage to take risks" when you occasionally fail.

197

"The solution suggested is certainly interesting," rather than "really weird."

"I'll choose to laugh" rather than anguish over some frustration.

"I'm going to take charge of my feelings" rather than being overwhelmed by them.

In short, make your self-instructions work for you, not against you.

PRETENDING YOU'RE SOMEONE ELSE

If you ever played with dolls as a child, you will remember the fascination of imagining yourself as someone else. In this case we are not trying to imitate behavior but to view the world through different eyes in order to restructure our thinking.

Bev is 28, supports herself, and lives with her boyfriend in a small apartment several miles from her parents. They are her problem. "Growing up I usually conformed to their wishes and really gave them practically no trouble at all. Our relationship was good until about eight months ago when Rick moved in with me. They just can't accept our living together without being married. It isn't as if I'm dependent upon them. I'm grown up and want to lead my own life in my own way, but they won't let me. I get so mad at them sometimes I'm like a little kid with a temper tantrum. Then I feel guilty. After all, I do love my parents."

One of the ways Bev works on the problem with her parents is to imagine how she would talk with them if she were not their daughter but another older person, even though her parents, not knowing she is doing this, would still relate to her as a daughter. She imagines how she would react differently to them as someone less involved and more experienced, a person not emotionally torn by parental resistance and with less need to define her own autonomy.

Though it is impossible for Bev to remain consistently in the role of the other person, she does find that with concentration she is able to attain a more dispassionate stand with her parents than before. While they don't change their minds, it does help Bev and her parents come closer to an acceptance of their differences. By changing "where she is coming from" Bev slows a vicious cycle of accusations and anger.

B. J. is a complainer. No doubt about it. And she knows it, too. She is unhappy with her life, but her inertia keeps her from doing anything about it. She seems to gain enough satisfaction from grumbling to others to continue. But her negativism does concern her, and finally she asks herself this question: "What am I going to be like twenty years down the line if I keep this up?" She shudders.

With an outside assist, this question sets the stage for imagery that helps B. J. restructure her thinking. "I imagined myself a bitchy old woman. No one liked me. People talked about me behind my back and went out of their way to walk around me as if I had some contagious disease. I never had visitors. My family wouldn't even phone me long-distance on weekends, nights, or holidays when there were special rates."

At first B. J. does not try to change herself. For one week she simply spends a few minutes each day with the imagery just described. But the following week when she sets about deliberately cutting down on her negativism, she switches her imagery to a sequence of events twenty years later in which all the happiness not present in the first imagery *is* present, including loving long-distance calls from friends during peak rate hours. For B. J., imagery alone is not likely to restructure totally her negative thinking, but it can help.

Try this some time. When you are in a place where others don't know you, maybe in a department store or when you are on a trip alone, imagine yourself as another you. Deliberately act differently. The new you might give the old you ideas for starter goals you hadn't dreamed of.

THINKING DIFFERENTLY
DUE TO CHANGED SURROUNDINGS

You recall that in Chapter eight we discussed how our surroundings serve as cues to the roles we play in life. Laurel, a divorced woman supporting a child, understands this when she starts a tax consulting business in her own home. She says she wants to cut down on the time she spends thinking about housework and cooking while she works in the office part of her house. "Specifically, I want to encourage my image of myself as a career person, especially since my job takes place at home."

Though she can ill afford to do so, Laurel arranges for housecleaning help one afternoon a week with an evening meal to be cooked by the person who comes. She sees this combination as the one most likely to tie her to her office after lunch and not let her break early for dinner. Her hope is that working this plan one day a week will set a precedent for firmer work patterns the other days.

With just one change in her surroundings, Laurel begins to think of herself more as a career woman and less as a homemaker.

COMBINATIONS

Once we become successful focusing our attention on irrational self-thoughts we can work with many self-change ideas. Marilyn, for example, selects several to help her with the auto mechanics course. Combining a fear-reduction hierarchy of small steps to help her feel more comfortable attending class with personal cueing to counter her negative self-statements, she also makes certain that she elicits strong, reinforcing support from friends. "They really took the course with me, in absentia." Marilyn ended up attending eight of her ten auto mechanics classes.

Taking charge of the messages we give ourselves helps us restructure our thinking. Then self-sabotaging thoughts no longer hold us back. In their revised forms they move us forward.

Part 5

PURSUING
A PERSPECTIVE

You know now how to make your own changes and what changes the women in this book view as important for themselves. Chapter fourteen summarizes what we have shared with a look toward the future.

CHAPTER FOURTEEN

Final Steps
and Future Stakes

I am making myself known to me. It's like
developing a friendship with anyone else. We've been
acquaintances for a long time, but now I think we
stand a pretty good chance of becoming close friends.

Melanie

I finally understand. All kinds of outside forces
impinge on me unless I am aware of what they are
and, through my own strength, equalize the pressures—
or reverse them. No one in the world can do that for
me. I'm on my own.

Pam

The Self-Change Principles:
Parts That Fit Together

Now that you have a working understanding of the ten behavioral principles, you will find they make sense as a consistent whole with all of the pieces fitting together. For
example, you see that the notion of a hierarchy not only helps
you overcome stress or fear but is the reason for identifying
target behaviors and recognizing any small achievements as

you go along; that surrounding cues not only prepare you to begin a new behavior but to stop one that you don't like; and that your own imagination not only creates fantasy but is a tool to help you rehearse, reward, and project to other roles. These kinds of insights give you a broader perspective, allowing you to apply the methods in ways unrestricted by the three main categories that served to introduce them to you. Here, then, are the principles all together.

THE BEHAVIORAL SELF-CHANGE PRINCIPLES*

1. **The Starter Goal Principle:** To determine the action you want to take, restate a global goal in operational terms as several starter goals and then convert each starter goal into precise target behaviors you can work on in given situations.

2. **The Fear/Stress Principle:** To help overcome fear or tension about a situation, very gradually increase your exposure to the situation while you are otherwise relaxed, secure, and rewarded.

3. **The Reinforcement Principle:** To initiate or strengthen an action, reinforce it (or any tendencies toward it) as soon as possible following each improved performance until that action is learned.

4. **The Modeling Principle:** To learn a new way of responding, observe a (prestigious) person who performs a behavior you want to learn and use that person as your example.

5. **The Cueing Principle:** To strengthen or develop a new action, note the situational cues immediately preceding the present action and change them to other conditions that prompt the behavior you desire.

6. **The Satiation Principle:** To stop a certain action, allow or insist that the behavior continue until fatigue or boredom sets in to end it.

7. **The Extinction Principle:** To stop a certain action, make sure no rewards follow it.

8. **The Incompatible Alternative Principle:** To stop any action, reward an alternative behavior that is inconsistent with or cannot be performed at the same time as the one you wish to end.

9. **The Negative Reinforcement Principle:** To stop a certain action, end a mildly punishing situation immediately when the behavior improves.

*Adapted from John D. and Helen B. Krumboltz, *Changing Children's Behavior*, © 1972, pp. 232–233. By permission of Prentice-Hall, Englewood Cliffs, N.J.

10. **The Countering Principle:** To stop a self-sabotaging action, focus on specific ways you give yourself irrational messages and change those messages to ones of self-support.

The Behavioral
Self-Change Contract

With certain of our principles we mentioned ways other people might assist while we remain in control of our change project. Here is a final possibility. Now that you are familiar with all of the principles, the self-change contract, on the next page, will incorporate any ideas from the principles of your choice.

Note that because of the way it is constructed the contract utilizes behavioral methods of its own: It assures that we state precisely the change we wish to make, spell out the details for accomplishing the change, and decide on definite time constraints. It also reserves space for two signatures: our own and that of a witness.

The witness plays a key role. First, another person involved usually gives us a stronger commitment. We feel additional responsibility for following through. Second, the witness can serve as a source of reinforcement for us, emphasizing our improvements and carefully avoiding reacting to our delays in the ways we've described earlier. If you want this kind of help, choose an understanding person. You may even decide to have two witnesses instead of one.

A variation of this contract is one in which two people serve as witnesses and potential sources of reinforcement for each other. It's an "I'll-reward-you-for-this-if-you-reward-me-for-that" agreement by both parties, put into writing.

Self-change contracts are short-term and pertain to limited, achievable goals. To be successful they must be realistic.

Women's Starter Goals:
Two Challenges

When we tie down the abstractions and obstructions in our lives, we find many starter goals women have in common

```
┌─────────────────────────────────────────────────────────────┐
│  SELF-CHANGE CONTRACT                                         │
│  Effective dates: From _____ to _____                     │
│                                                               │
│  I, _____ agree to _____  │
│  _____    │
│  (make starter goal clear)                                    │
│                                                               │
│  in the following situation(s): _____ │
│  _____    │
│  (make target behavior(s) specific: place, time, persons, etc.)│
│                                                               │
│  _____    │
│                                                               │
│  I plan to accomplish this by _____ │
│  _____    │
│  (indicate application(s) of specific principle(s))           │
│                                                               │
│  _____    │
│                                                               │
│  _____    │
│                                                               │
│  Reward(s) provided by myself or others, assuming contract is kept: │
│  _____    │
│                                                               │
│  _____    │
│                                                               │
│                              _____ │
│                                              (my signature)   │
│  _____                _____ │
│  (date)                                (witness's signature)  │
└─────────────────────────────────────────────────────────────┘
```

because of socialization. In Chapter two a number of women
shared their starter goals with you, and as you think of your
own you most likely will share yours with others. However,
our challenge is twofold: not only to find our starter goals,

but to be ingenious in applying the self-change methods so they cease being our *goals* and start to become our *realities*. Then we really know we are *getting there*.

Men's Starter Goals: Their Own Challenge

Men who seek a life style in harmony with women's recently expressed needs often confront a society that instead offers them rewards for continuing to act in the same old ways. Some of these rewards come from women themselves who give their own mixed messages. A woman may ask herself, "Would I really be attracted to a man who doesn't want to live so competitively, is open about his dependency needs, or is willing to share power?" Yet as women understandably disturb the old equilibrium to seek greater equity and personal growth, it is clear that any new equilibrium involves changes for men as well. Now men have an opportunity to examine their own roles, for although they are recipients of more blessings in our society than women, they bear their own burdens.

As their awareness grows, some men also work on starter goals and target behaviors for self-change. For example, they may examine their areas of stress and fears, often related to job performance since traditionally success for men is so narrowly defined by their work. They may look more closely at their personal lives and move toward more nurturing relationships with others (a male friend, a father, a wife, a child). They may stop to ponder and question the ways they have been socialized regarding women, perhaps playing the protector role to the detriment of their own personal growth, or perceiving us primarily as sex objects. Like women, men have many options for potential change and are responsible for their own decisions. The same kinds of resources women use for finding starter goals are available to them, and our self-change principles harbor no sex bias.

The Real You:
An Original

Today we live on the cutting edge of social change for women. We have a choice: We can look upon this change as one that creates dilemmas, resistance, and confusion, or as one that creates new visions and new opportunities for women and men alike. Naturally we prefer the latter.

Viewing current social change as an opportunity for special growth, we have looked at the dilemmas and aspirations of many different women. And we have looked closely at ourselves and our surroundings. Like Pam and Melanie at the beginning of this chapter, we realize how crucial it is to increase our awareness of who *we* are as individuals and of the impact on us of our personal environment. Pam concludes, "No one else can do that for me. I'm on my own." We're *all* on our own—and that's important to remember.

We have a vision of the real you (which is, of course, the real us and the real me). In this vision people say: "She exudes self-esteem." "She has a definite sense of who she is, of her own identity." "No smashing anger or destructive guilt in her." "She deals positively with people around her." "You can tell she's in charge of her life." These descriptions reflect our global goals, and we have shown ways women can work toward attaining them.

You are an original. As you select self-change projects, you chart your own directions using your own unique talents and skills, keeping in mind your particular needs and desires. You work with your own potentialities.

Increasingly you become—the *real* you. You are *getting there.* And as you do, you create an aura of your own. You generate your own mystique.

Index

Relaxation exercises, 72–75
  instant, 74–75
  progressive, 72–74
Resistance
  from family, 10
  from self, 13
  strengthened in extinction, 166
Responses
  counting, 44–46
  minimal, 161–62
  neutral, 155, 159–61
Rewards. *See* Gratifications, Positive reinforcement, Praise; Tangible rewards.
Risk-taking, 9, 13, 97
Role models. *See* Modeling, Models, sources of.
Role playing. *See also* Rehearsal in hierarchies, 80.
  with satiation, 147–48
  in try-out roles, 133

Satiation, 143–53
  cautions, 152–53
    possible harm, 152
    possible reinforcement, 152–53
  never with extinction, 164
  stopping others' actions, 150–52
  stopping own actions, 145–50
    ending avoidance, 150
    blocks in thinking, 149–50
    habitual errors, 149
    pent-up feelings, 146–47
    excessive habits, 147–49
  principles, 145
  Time for Yourself project, 153
Self-awareness, 10 See also Identity, personal
Self-change contract, 205
Self-cueing, 121–129. *See also* Cueing of others.
  automated self-cueing, 129
  double take method, 116–19
  with imagery, 129
  self-instruction, 127–28, 187–90

reacting to others' cues, 138–39
  determining correct cue, 139
  making own decision, 139
  labeling, 139
  rechecking response, 139
principle, 127
sources of cues, 122–26
  body cues, 124–25
  negative consequences, 125–26
  person cues, 122
  place cues, 122–23
  positive consequences, 125
  self-prophecy cues, 123–24
  time cues, 123
thought stopping, 123
Time for Yourself project, 129
Self-deception, 13. *See also* Self-sabotage.
Self-esteem, 10, 20, 23, 55–56, 163, 208
  starter goals:
    fears limiting, 27
    actions promoting, 29–30
    actions restricting, 33
Self-instructions. *See also* Self-sabotage, Self-statements.
  changing, 197–98
  faulty, 187–90
Self-nurturance, 12, 55–56, 87–88, 129. *See also* Countering; Positive reinforcement.
Self-monitoring, 38–53
  advantages:
    noting other influences, 41
    measuring own actions, 41
    comparing stereotypic behavior to own, 39–41
  data-collecting methods, 42–53
  examples of:
    approval needs, 40
    arguments with husband, 48–49
    dependency on others, 49–50
    feelings of depression, 46–47
    giving honest positive feedback, 43

216